The Road Less Traveled

My Journey to Monkhood

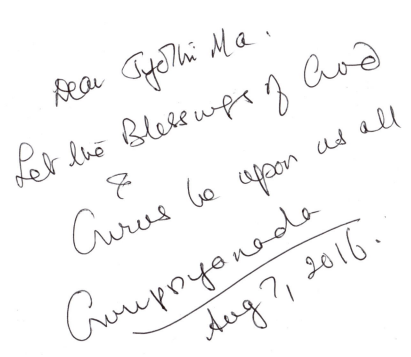

Dear Jyothi Ma.
Let the Blessings of God
&
Gurus be upon us all
Gurupriyananda
Aug 7, 2016.

Swami Gurupriyananda Giri

The Road Less Traveled
My Journey to Monkhood

©Sudha Bathina

First Edition 2014

ISBN:978-0-692-27402-6

Srividya Publications

DEDICATION

To Paramahamsa Prajnanananda,
my guru and guide on the journey
toward enlightenment.

Humble
Gurupriyananda

ACKNOWLEDGEMENTS

I wish to thank Swami Matrukrupananda Giri, previously Dr. Harinath Bathina, who supported and accompanied me wholeheartedly on this journey to a common destination.

I am immensely thankful to Dr. Jyothi Bathina, who spent countless hours helping me polish, edit, and organize my thoughts and bring them into book form.

I wish to also profess my eternal gratitude to all the gurus and guides I have encountered on life's path. Each of them has taught me valuable lessons that have informed my choices on this journey.

Humble
Gurupriyananda

ABOUT THE AUTHOR

Swami Gurupriyananda Giri, formerly Sudha Bathina, is a practicing monk of the Prajnana Mission. She has traversed the four stages of life: from a *brahmacharini* with a postgraduate degree, to a *grihasthi* with a husband, three children and a teaching career, to a *vanaprasthi* living a life of service, and finally to a *sannyasi* under the guidance of her beloved guru Paramahamsa Prajnanananda. She now spends her time between the U.S. and India ashrams in meditation, study, teaching and service. She is the editor of *Sthita Prajna,* a quarterly journal of the Prajnana Mission.

FOREWORD

I have been waiting for this book. A few years ago, I was urging Sudha Ma to write a book on our beloved Guruji, Paramahamsa Prajnanananda Baba, knowing that she would have much to tell. As I read this book, I am overwhelmed - little did I know of the richness of the treasure she would share with us - about Guruji, and about her own journey. In all my years of association with Guruji, it has been a joy to read and hear about Baba's love and devotion for Gurudev Paramahamsa Hariharananda Baba, and secretly in my heart I have also yearned for the day that someone would write just as effusively and lovingly about Guruji, Baba Prajnananandaji. This book fills that void.

Time stopped for me as I read the book - it was like being merged in meditation itself. The prologue was spell binding, the narrative fast-paced, and the many segues deftly woven into the fabric of her story. Memories of all the times spent with Guruji came flooding back - those feelings of pure love, reverence, gratitude, and blessedness that felt impossible to express in words. But as I read Ma's lucid narration of her own experiences - those feelings welled up again.

The countless people who have been touched and transformed by Baba will find their own experiences reverberate in their heart, as they read along, and they will also learn so much more about Baba from all the times they couldn't be with him. As I finished the book, the mind bowed down at the divine lotus feet of this great Master, just as we do after completing our meditation. I also bow down to Gurupriyananda Ma and Matrukrupananda Baba. For the legions of householder devotees of Guruji, I doubt if there are many others who stand out as such towering role models. Where they are at now is truly on a road less traveled, and not many of us will get there. But however far we get, their journey of sadhana, dedication, love, and transformation will always be an inspiration. This book will itself be a great reference for what it means to be the ideal devotees of a God realized and divine Master.

Humbly,

Amit Chatterjee
Partner Developer
Microsoft

PREFACE

The seed for wanting to write something about my time with Baba was sown in the year 2002, after Baba's publication of *River of Compassion* and *My time with the Master*, which documented the extraordinary life of Paramahamsa Hariharananda and Baba's own experiences with his Master. It is a blessing that God has bestowed on me to be able to spend time with the Baba during the times of his evolving and blossoming into a world teacher and expanding his mission. The humble wish rose within me to attempt to pay tribute to my own Guru as he had done with his.

Over the years, sincere disciples had approached me to write about my time with Baba. I had the good fortune of being close to his family and was able to collect some childhood incidents from talking to them and also from Baba's talks. A few of these appeared in *Sthita Prajna,* the quarterly journal of Prajnana Mission as *Prajnana Katha Sudha,* my early attempt at starting a biography of Baba. I soon realized, however, that except for dates and facts, one cannot really write about the Guru with such limited knowledge unless he reveals himself, which he rarely did.

What I started writing shaped itself into more of what I know of myself, my thoughts and my journey and growth in the company of the Guru and some lessons I have learned in the process. Writing this volume has given me great joy and fulfillment, not only for having known Baba and spending a good part of my time with him, but for having the opportunity to share that experience with others. So while I have not written a comprehensive biography of Baba, I have sought to pass on the experiences and reflections of one of his disciples in the hopes that it will serve to inspire others who follow the same path.

Humble,

Gurupriyananda

CONTENTS

PROLOGUE

On a cool February morning in 2012, by the banks of a tranquil pond in the Hariharananda Gurukulam in Odisha, India, I flung my body into the sacrificial fire and watched it burn. As the frail figure burst into flames, symbolizing my disintegrating attachment to my mortal shell, I felt none of the pain, remorse, fear, or attachment that people anticipate when renouncing the world and accepting a life of spiritual pursuit.

I had spent the day before bidding goodbye to all the gods of the Hindu pantheon that I had worshipped throughout my life, to the nine planets that had governed my destiny thus far, to the four directions and the four corners, and each of their respective rulers: Indra, Yama, Kubera and Varuna, to all my forefathers, both maternal and paternal, who had contributed to my birth, to all the saints and sages from Vasishtha to Viswamitra, from Adi Shankaracharya to Sathya Sai, who had established and upheld the vedic traditions I once revered.

I had spent the night chanting sacred mantras, purifying myself for the coming rebirth, the auspicious moment that comes in so few lives, after a lifetime of preparation, to relinquish all ties to the physical, emotional and spiritual forces that bind us while still alive and to choose the life of a monk, one who is no longer bound by any of the laws, natural, physical or social, that govern the lives of ordinary men and women.

The euphoria that swept through me that morning as I witnessed my own demise was beyond any happiness I had ever felt, as a child, as a young woman, as a wife or a mother. It was an ecstatic feeling of release and rejuvenation, a nameless bliss that enveloped me wholly and completely. Once my fellow initiates and I, including my husband, Harinath, had burned our symbolic bodies made of *kusha* grass in the fire, we lined up to have our heads shaved. Again, though a woman, I felt no sting of vanity as the barber ran his razor across my scalp, the long black locks falling silently to the ground. For the first time, I felt the thrilling fingers of the breeze as they stroked my bare head, leaving my scalp tingling and alive. No longer did I need to worry about coloring my hair, about covering the bald spots that increased with age, or the silvery gray that belied my years. I was free of all the frivolous worries and duties engendered by human vanity.

Newly shorn, we reassembled beside the pond, which served as a tranquil witness to our rebirth at the hands of our guru, Paramahamsa Prajnanananda. The still water reflected his slight figure, personally pouring buckets of *panchagavya* or cow products such as cow dung, cow urine, milk, curd, and ghee on our heads, purifying us further with the ancient Ayurvedic remedy. We then bathed and returned to the worship place, where we performed another fire ceremony, and were presented with our new saffron robes and a sturdy stick and a water pot. The *danda* (stick), the *jola* (bag) and *kamandalam* (water pot) represented our new status as mendicants, who having no possessions of our own, wandered the earth with no attachments and asked only for each day's alms and water.

Baba, which is how we referred to our guru, then went down the row of new initiates, presenting us each with our new names. It was a beautiful ceremony with no forethought involved, Baba gazed deeply into each of our eyes and the right name would come to him, which he then announced softly to each of us. My new name was Gurupriyananda, which means "one who finds bliss in being dear to the Guru." My husband was now Matrukrupananda "one who finds bliss in the Divine Mother's grace." Both names were perfectly apt, for my bliss for the past 14 years had been in following the teachings of the guru before me, and my husband had for decades been a sincere devotee of Mother Durga, who could lose himself for hours in contemplation and chanting of Her divine name.

Once we had received our new names, we visited the temple within the ashram grounds and received our first symbolic alms from the ashram guests, who dropped coins into our new *jola* or bag. After this symbolic initiation into the life of a monk, we visited the famous temple of Lord Jagannath of Puri and returned to the ashram. While begging would not actually be a part of our daily life, we returned knowing that the inner transformation and new attitude were meant to be permanent. No longer could we have selfish desires or pray for personal gain. All our thoughts from this day forward were to be directed for the benefit of mankind and for the pursuit of salvation. We belonged now only to God and Guru, and he was as responsible for our future conduct as we were responsible for living up to the incredibly high standards expected of those who live wholly for others.

On that auspicious night of Sivaratri, as we continued our nightlong vigil in the temple dedicated to the very first yogi and renunciate, Lord Siva himself, I leaned against the cool stone wall and looked back at the path that had led me and my husband to this joyous common destiny, paved on its circuitous route by the love and guidance of our beloved guru.

With Gurudev Paramahamsa Hariharananda at Miami Ashram

1

FIRST STEPS TOWARD
KRIYA YOGA

During my Master's program at Osmania University, in Hyderabad, India, I met a young man who was finishing his Ph.D. in chemistry. Tall and lanky, he introduced himself as Harinath Bathina, a distant relative. From that day on, he would make some excuse or another to speak to me, or would walk back and forth in the hallways while I was attending class, or would offer to carry my books as I made my way from the building to the bus stop. Though I rebuffed his advances at first, he eventually endeared himself to me with his humor, his charm, and his persistence.

In fact, he became my unofficial bodyguard during the next two years, escorting me to and from classes and shielding me from the catcalls and eve teasing that went on in every co-ed college in India in those days. During the two years of study, we became good friends, and he eventually spoke to my father regarding my hand in marriage. With the consent of both our families, we had a grand wedding during the summer of 1962, just after my final exams for my master's degree in chemistry.

I was married into a good family. My in-laws were also of a firm religious and spiritual background, although they did not perform the elaborate rituals we engaged in at my parents' home.

By June of that same year, I was appointed as a lecturer in chemistry in a women's college, while my husband continued his Ph.D. program at the university. We were living in a joint family with my in-laws and many brothers-in-law. They were seven brothers and one sister all together. The youngest was my husband's sister Damayanti, who was barely three years old at the time of our wedding. All of them lived at home, except the eldest brother Kasinath. I basically ended up shifting from one big family into another after my marriage, since I had also grown up in a large family with five siblings and many cousins.

Although there were servants to help at my in-laws, it was still quite a challenge. I often had to cook when the cook was absent or wash the dishes when needed. I also worked full time and was raising my own three children, who were born in quick succession over the next few years. In addition, there were always relatives who came from the outer districts and who stayed on for days, thanks to the generosity of my father-in-law.

I was the first daughter-in-law and first young woman in the house and I was treated very well, like a daughter. Although my mother-in-law Smt. Sasirekha was not educated beyond the fifth grade, she was an extremely intelligent woman who ran the house efficiently and commanded the respect and devotion of all her children, her husband, and her relatives from near and far.

My father-in-law Bathina Ramachandra Rao was of a very charitable nature and took care of anybody and everybody that came for help. He was the legal advisor to the Criminal Investigation Department of Police at the time and had a good reputation as a lawyer. He loved his children and grandchildren immensely, and loved having his house full of relatives and friends, those who needed help, who were in town on business, or the countless people who came to him for advice. There would always be a pot of rice simmering on the stove to feed any who entered their doorway for any reason. As a result, my in-laws were much loved by many people.

My husband Harinath had a big heart, a generous, compassionate nature, and was particularly attached to his parents and family. He felt that his parents were to be treated as Parvati and Parmeshwar, the eternal couple of Siva and Shakti, yin and yang, power and consciousness, and we should do our best to serve and honor them.

I fit very well into the role of ideal daughter-in-law, taking care of the younger children, helping out in the kitchen and working outside the home. Since ours was not a traditionally arranged marriage, we started out as good friends, and adjusting to marriage was a smoother transition for me than most.

My husband had his flaws, he was known for his short temper, and was especially sensitive to anyone suffering. He could not tolerate a sad face, or even momentary depression, and rather than consoling the person, would explode at them, since he felt helpless to fix the problem. On the whole though, he was a loving husband and a good father, who never restricted my freedom. My economic independence from the very beginning definitely contributed to that freedom, so that despite living in a large family where all income was pooled into the common pot, we had some spare cash for our own enjoyment.

Raising a Family

At the time, except for praying to God on festival days and making an annual pilgrimage to Tirupati, Harinath was not too much into formal worship, preferring to be prayerful in silence,

Wedding

Young Family

21

In-Laws, Ramachandra Rao and Sesirekha

Parents, Ram Mohan and Bhagyavati with Srinath

reading, and contemplation. My father-in-law, Ramachandra Rao, had a special relationship with Lord Venkateswara. He would perform a five-minute *puja* or prayer each morning without fail, distributing the rock candy he offered as *prasad* to each family member when he was done. He had another special ritual that demonstrated his very personal relationship with God. There was a picture of Lord Venkateswara in the main hall of the house, and he would stand in front of it before he left for the office, discussing all his special requests and prayers. "Please get Harinath Babu his degree, and let my case go well today in court."

As we passed back and forth through the hall, we would see him standing there, dressed in his black law robes and stiff white shirt collar, speaking softly to the deity in the framed painting, asking advice, enlisting help, requesting favors, expressing gratitude, as easily and comfortably as if he were a trusted family member rather than a distant God. I always envied my father-in-law and later my husband and my daughter's ability to relate to God in this personal manner, as an advisor, a friend, and a confidante.

Within the first year of our marriage, our first and only daughter was born, and we named her Jyothi. The first grandchild in the family, she was loved and pampered by grandparents and uncles and aunts on both sides. She was highly intelligent, and I sent her to school early, at the age of two and a half. Chubby, with thick curly hair and short tight taffeta gowns, her plump little arms would barely reach around her father's waist as she sat behind him on his motorcycle and went back and forth between grandparents' houses.

After Jyothi's arrival, two more children were born to us, each two years apart, both boys, and named Muralinath and Srinath, in keeping with the tradition started by my father-in-law of ending all male children's names with nath. Our eldest son was a beautiful child, with fair skin and large, liquid eyes. He was my husband's favorite, holding the special place that eldest sons seem to have.

When Srinath, my third child was born, I was especially struck by the wise knowing look in his infant eyes. I was taken aback at first by his piercing stare, which seemed to be aware and focused like that of an adult, and not like the wide-eyed gaze of a newborn. Within the first few hours though, the look wore off, and he transformed into an innocent baby with round eyes and a hungry belly. Still I could not shake the feeling that Srinath had initially retained some memory of his past life and was aware and resigned to the fact that he had been reborn.

They say that each time we are reborn, we have full memory of all that has come before and of our impending birth, but that we lose that memory as we pass through the birth canal. In those first few minutes, it seemed to me that Srinath was sizing me up as his future mother before he relinquished that last shred of awareness and lapsed into his new life. Over the years, he ended up being a loyal and devoted son, always looking out for his parents and siblings.

Settling in the United States

Nearly two decades later, we arrived in the United States from India. We had visited before, staying for a few years each time, but on this our third visit, we intended to settle here for good.

Our daughter Jyothi was newly married, and we wanted to get the new couple settled here as well. We sent our sons Murali and Srinath to live temporarily with my sister Radha and her husband Ravi, who were now doctors in Fort Wayne, Indiana, while we moved back to the Chicago area to work.

It was during this time that the Hindu Temple of Chicago was being constructed, and it was a great experience to be fully involved with every step until the temple was complete. It was also very hard work, since Harinath was the treasurer of the executive committee of the temple. My husband was always drawn to temples and spent many years serving temples in the different cities we lived in.

We met several beautiful gurus over the years, such as Swami Bhashyananda of the Vivekananda Vedanta Society of Chicago, and we regularly attended their programs every Sunday at the Vedanta Society. Swami Ranganathananda, who later became the president of Ramakrishna Mission, used to visit the Vedanta Society from time to time and we attended some retreats in Ganges, Michigan.

Swami Dayananda Saraswati of the Arshavidya Gurukulam visited our home on one of his visits, as did Swami Vidyananda Giri of the Vyasashram, in India. We were fortunate to have all these holy men visit our homes in different places on different occasions. We made it a point to learn from all of them and were grateful for their blessings.

Over the years, Jyothi completed her Ph.D, Murali completed his M.D, and Srinath completed his M.B.A. Murali married a very nice girl, Jori, an occupational therapist from a loving and family oriented background whom he met while attending medical school. They moved out to Seattle and later to Boise, Idaho, and settled there, where Murali became head of his own cardiology practice. Srinath moved to California and began working in a management position at Intel. He eventually met and married Zenaida, a very spiritual young woman from the Philippines. Our children were grown up and settled in their lives. Our active parenting role, while never completely over, was coming to a natural and satisfactory completion.

Eventually, tired of working in isolation at my initial job in a chemistry lab, I decided to try my hand at real estate. A successful realtor friend of mine advised me to capitalize on my many connections in the Indian community. The market was booming at the time and I obtained my realtor license and sold millions of dollars worth of inventory within a year. I thoroughly enjoyed working as a realtor. Even more than the commission, I took pleasure in making the sale, finding the right home for each family, and getting to know them during the process. After years of working on my own in various labs and living within the narrow circle of family and friends, I began to enjoy the experience of getting to know more and more people. I was exposed to different personalities, different ways of thinking, and different family structures. It was fascinating and just as much fun to observe as the experiments I relished in my research days.

It was during this period that I first began wearing makeup. Lipstick apparently was a must for a realtor, and I also had my hair cut short and permed, began to drive a Mercedes and then a Cadillac, had a business card with a professional portrait, and worked in a realtor's office with a secretary.

Unfortunately, the market fell and we were saddled with two large mansions that we had invested in, hoping to turn them around for a profit. At the time, my husband Harinath was the Director of Research and Quality Control at a chemical company in Chicago. When the company closed, he had to move to Charlotte, North Carolina, to take a job in order to keep up with the outrageous mortgages on both houses.

I stayed behind in Chicago, living in one of the homes and trying hard to sell both. I felt quite a bit of guilt for having convinced my husband that the houses were a good investment. After a year of struggle, we were able to sell both for a slight loss but the relief was tremendous. After that neither of us was interested in business ventures any longer, content to live within our means and leave speculation and risk taking to others.

Looking back, it was a period when greed and the desire for material success led to struggle and unnecessary stress in our lives. The need to put on a false facade, to put on blusher and lipstick, to drive ostentatious cars, were all a part of this drive to succeed at any cost. I was relieved to drop all those affectations and move on.

Discovering the Path of Yoga

One day during his year in Charlotte, as he was browsing through a spiritual bookstore, Harinath found the book *Autobiography of a Yogi* by Paramahamsa Yogananda, the founder of Self Realization Fellowship. He was greatly impressed by the book, which describes how Yogananda vigorously pursued his spiritual journey with great conviction, hours of meditation and strict discipline. Sharing Yogananda's love for the Divine Mother, my husband immediately signed up for an 18-month correspondence course with Self Realization Fellowship.

After that year, Harinath moved back to Chicago to start in a new position. He flew to L.A. to visit the S.R.F. center and participated in some of the meditations. However, while the devotion of S.R.F. members to their departed master was inspiring, we were still in search of a *sadguru,* or a teacher in human form, who could be our living guide.

Durga Ma, a friend of ours from Chicago, was a disciple of Paramahamsa Hariharananda, a great yogi and a fellow disciple of Paramahamsa Yogananda. The two Paramahamsas had both studied under Shriyukteshwar, a revered teacher of the Kriya Yoga lineage. While Yogananda had moved to the West much earlier and established S.R.F., Hariharananda had remained in India for many years teaching Kriya, only traveling to the West in 1974, when he was 67 years old. He eventually established ashrams in both Europe and the United States.

The U.S. ashram was sending out disciples to various cities to hold programs and establish centers. Durga Ma invited us to a Kriya program that was being held in Chicago and my husband took his first initiation in the year 1990.

Four years later, my husband accepted a new position in Cleveland. Despite being immersed in religious ritual and *puja*, as well as the study of scriptures until that time, I began feeling the need for meditation and thought I would try Kriya Yoga, as my husband liked the practice. At that time, I joined a Gita study group in Cleveland, where I met a lady who was practicing meditation. She was also interested in Kriya Yoga and told us there was a program scheduled in Chicago where we could be initiated. The venue turned out to be none other than our old friend Durga Ma's house. My husband and I joined a few interested people from Cleveland and made the trip back to Chicago to be initiated into Kriya Yoga. We were joined there by my sister Radha and her husband Ravi. They were also initiated at the same time.

During the process of initiation, we were introduced to the fascinating science behind Kriya. It is a scientific technique of meditation that teaches channeling the *prana* through the seven chakras in the spine in order to achieve soul consciousness through sincere meditation and concentration. Chakras are the energy centers or the subtle forces that energize the physical body. Kriya is a combination of many exercises that help in the control of breath and physical metabolism without any strain.

Kriya Yoga is a science that plays on the connection between the breath and the mind. We learned that by controlling the breath, we could regulate our mind, our thoughts and our ego, and therefore proceed more easily on the path of spirituality. Kriya Yoga is taught directly by the guru to the disciple and involves a purification process and energization of the chakras through which one perceives divine sound, light and vibration.

I was amazed that what was taught in Kriya Yoga was so strongly based on the chakras, something we were first introduced to in the worship of the Divine Mother. We had spent many years in her worship after searching for a path to God in our younger days.

❊ ❊ ❊ ❊ ❊ ❊ ❊ ❊ ❊ ❊ ❊ ❊ ❊ ❊ ❊ ❊ ❊ ❊ ❊

The Divine Mother

In the late 70's, when our children were still in their teens and we were living in India, Harinath was the Head of Research and Development for Indian Detonators Limited in Hyderabad. He managed 120 chemists in his group and took three or four trips a year to Europe or the United States. All expenses were paid. Travel was in style with first-class train and plane tickets and we stayed in five star hotels or in company guesthouses in Delhi, Bangalore, Bombay and Stockholm. For all this material success and comfort, my husband still felt that something was missing. The desire to see God was intense. He felt a little helpless. He didn't know how to pray or what to say and he didn't know any mantras.

One weekend in Delhi, we walked from our guesthouse up a small hill to a Siva-Parvati temple. We sat there and prayed intensely for some direction. We gained a clearer picture of what we needed to do, and from that day on we both became vegetarian and started praying to Lord Siva.

This is the time when Harinath started his own search for a chosen deity. His interest was triggered on a Mahasivaratri day. On that day, we performed an elaborate *abhishekham* or bathing ritual of Lord Siva in a temple. The priest was a great devotee of Lord Siva and the way he performed the ritual, with the chanting of the *rudram*, left us with an intensely purifying and inspiring experience. It was also a time when we were visiting many temples and felt the urge to be able to sing and praise the Lord, but did not know any mantra or prayers.

Listening to the *rudram,* a hymn which reverentially invokes the Lord's presence and sings of His glory, we felt an inner communion with the Lord that we had not perceived before. The experience also left us with a heightened sense of the Shakti and presence of the Divine Mother, combined with a subtle sense of deep familiarity, as if we had listened to this *rudram* many times before. Maybe it was an impression left over from previous lives. At that point, my husband began to consider who his *ishta devata* or his chosen deity should be. After reflecting deeply on who would be the ultimate manifestation of Divine Power and Energy, he chose the Divine Mother.

Sri Ramachandra Murthy

In his search for a proper guide in the worship of the Mother, Harinath consulted with our family priest, Sambhiah, who suggested we meet Sri Ramachandra Murthy to be initiated with a mantra. Our search for a guru for mantra initiation thus led us to Brahmasri Ramachandra Murthy, who was a great worshipper of the Divine Mother in the form of Devi Lalitha. He was also a great devotee of Lord Rama. He was an orthodox brahmin, a householder with wife and children, who worked as a chartered accountant, but was also a very spiritual person. He had some spiritual powers, although he did not advertise them. He was a scholar, well read in scriptures, as well as an astrologer, and was believed to have attained full power over the mantras, and knew the exact science of ritual worship. When we first went to him, he was hesitant to give us instruction, as he said one had to be really disciplined to be able to worship Lalitha. But seeing my husband's persistence, he said, "If you are really determined, first learn how to do the *sahasranama* with proper pronunciation. Come every Sunday to my place and join in the chanting."

Every Sunday, Sri Ramachandra Murthy held a meeting to worship Devi Lalitha with the chanting of *sahasranama,* which extols the thousand names and qualities of the Goddess. In this sacred hymn there is a section that refers to the worship of the Mother as the energy residing in the chakras or the lotuses along the spine and also as traveling through the *susushmna* channel in the spine from the *muladhara* to *sahasrara* to unite with the soul residing there, exactly what is referred to in Kriya Yoga.

Many people gathered at Ramachandra Murthy's house to attend the worship, and then waited for his blessing when he put the *kumkum*, the sacred red powder offered to Devi, on their foreheads. Many also came to have diseases cured, or for solutions to problems, which they believed he could solve with the help of the Divine Mother. So we went every Sunday for a few Sundays, and when he was satisfied we could recite the hymn properly, he gave us another test. He asked Harinath to do the *sahasranama*

Sri Ramachandra Murthy

Harinath Consecrating Chandi Idol

a hundred times and then come back to him. With great determination, my husband completed this task, spending most Sundays for hours in the prayer room.

We thus officially started Devi worship from the late 70's under Sri Ramachandra Murthy's guidance. We performed the *sahasranama* every day, but Friday evenings were very special. We fasted all day and then cooked a feast, which was offered to Devi after the evening worship. It was almost like a festival each week.

Later, pleased with Harinath's persistence and discipline, Ramachandra Murthy asked both of us to come for initiation on an auspicious day. He gave each of us three mantras and explained how to chant them. This was our first formal initiation into a mantra.

By now, we understood that Devi was the energy of God and was inseparable from him. Harinath's favorite mantra was of *chandi* and over the years, he chanted it several million times, amassing what he considers his greatest wealth. Whenever there was a need in the family, Ramachandra Murthy always gave him a mantra to chant for removing the problem. Eventually when Ramachandra Murthy established a temple in Hyderabad, we sponsored the Chandi Idol. Harinath carried the idol into the temple himself, having purified and prepared himself for the sacred task by performing over nine lakhs of chandi japa.

For Harinath, the most comfortable way to be close to God was to do *puja* and *japa*. No intellectual understanding or interpretation of inner meanings was necessary, just a simple and straightforward love for God. He was a priest at heart. That is what he knew best and loved the most. At the time, we were both performing external worship using flowers, fruits, different kinds of food, and offerings.

✳ ✳ ✳ ✳ ✳ ✳ ✳ ✳ ✳ ✳ ✳ ✳ ✳ ✳ ✳ ✳ ✳ ✳ ✳

Now that we had been introduced to Kriya, we were learning that the same worship could be performed internally using the breath to energise the chakras along the spine. It was as though, pleased with our years of dedicated worship, the Divine Mother directed us to this path of Kriya Yoga, to go inward as the next step in our *sadhana* or practice. The lineage of the Kriya Masters was inspiring. Following initiation, I longed to meet the *sadguru*, the living Master, in person.

Meeting the Master

In September 1996, the same group of people from Cleveland traveled to Florida to meet Paramahamsa Hariharananda. The Kriya Yoga ashram in Florida was then located in a rented house. By the time we reached the ashram, morning meditation was already complete. Gurudev Hariharananda had just finished his lunch and was resting. Although we were very anxious to see him, we were not sure if we could. One of the brahmacharis went into Gurudev's room to enquire. He returned with a smile and to our delight, said we could go in and meet him.

We entered with trepidation to see Gurudev lying on his bed, a picture of love and compassion with his glowing complexion and divine aura. He greeted us warmly with a beaming smile and said, "Please come in." Though he was fatigued, he received each one of us as we came forward and knelt by his bed, and blessed us by vigorously rubbing each of our heads. We sat around his bed for a while as he related incidents from his youth. As I gazed at him, I could see a brilliant white light emanating from his body. It was whiter than the white sheet he was lying on and it extended all the way to the wall behind his bed. To be in the presence of this realized yogi, so humble and childlike, had a tremendous effect.

During that visit there was another young monk with Gurudev, who was also there for the first time. He did not talk much at the time but his face was so radiant with spiritual energy and glowing with such love, that we were irresistibly drawn to him. I remember my husband saying, "This swami is not ordinary." I was reminded of Paramahamsa Yogananda for some reason. I do not remember any conversation with him, but learned that his name was Swami Prajnanananda. He was with Gurudev all the time and the only word we heard him speak as a reply to anything that Gurudev said was "Baba" in a tone that meant, "Yes." He conducted the meditation that evening along with Gurudev as well as the initiations the next morning. He took great care to make sure each of us perceived the triple divine qualities of light, sound and vibration during our meditation.

Curious to know more about him, we made some inquiries and pieced together his history. Born Triloki Dash to an illustrious brahmin family in Odisha, he had always been drawn to the spiritual path and would often visit the Himalayas and spiritual teachers even as a youth. In his sincere quest for a guru, he met and was immediately accepted as a disciple by Paramahamsa Hariharananda, who saw great potential and divinity in the young man.

Triloki Dash completed his postgraduate degree in Economics and worked as a professor at Ravenshaw College in Cuttack while staying at the ashram, serving his guru, and conducting his own spiritual sadhana. He originally intended to complete his Ph.D. but Gurudev, who recognized the potential of his new disciple, soon made him a monk, assuring him that his purpose was much greater and more far reaching. He was chosen to spread Gurudev's word both in India and abroad.

Little did I know at the time when we first met him in Florida, that this illustrious young monk was to be our mentor, guide and spiritual teacher, the guru I had been searching for, whose touch transformed the whole family and changed our lives forever.

2

THE ARRIVAL OF THE GURU

We returned elated to Cleveland from our Florida trip, and eventually we were chosen to host the Cleveland Kriya Yoga Center. We were living in Hudson, Ohio, and our first Kriya program in Cleveland was to be held on a 4th of July weekend in 1997. We were informed by the main center in Florida that Swami Prajnanananda, the designated successor to Gurudev, would be arriving to lead our program.

A group of disciples had gathered in the house to welcome and meet him. He came in with a radiant smile, bowing to touch the threshold before entering the house. He stayed with us for four days. During those four days, time stood still. Words cannot describe the joy he spread around him. He radiated love in his walk, talk and every act. It must be the bliss and knowledge attained through the practice of Kriya Yoga or his compassion for humanity. It was not like anything I had ever seen. I told myself, "God has sent me my guru- a guru who can demonstrate how to love God in a practical way."

What we experienced during that time, I don't think I can aptly describe in words. The programs were a great success. In the introductory lecture on Kriya Yoga, Baba, as we began calling him, described both the science and the spirituality behind the

Early Days with the Guru

technique. Those who were not yet initiated formally were given initiation by Baba personally. We watched in wonder, as he purified each of the chakras in the spine with his energy and then made sure each person was able to experience the triple divine qualities of light, sound, and vibration on their own. We were overwhelmed by the love and humility with which he washed each person's feet and symbolically washed away their sins.

The guided meditations that followed were so inspiring, as Baba gently led us through the steps and helped us watch our breath. Many devotees would come both morning and evening for guided sessions and when the meditation was over, no one wanted to leave his presence. He would sit patiently for hours between sessions, answering our questions, and sharing stories from the lives of saints and the scriptures of both East and West to illustrate his points.

During that time, someone asked him "Baba, how do you do this? How can you give so much love to so many people?" His answer was, "It is simple. When I am with you, I am fully with you. If I get a phone call from Germany now and I have to talk to someone, I will be fully with them. When I am done, I am fully back to you. It is feeling God's presence in everything you do and doing it as God's work and with love for God." It sounds very simple, but just like the most basic precept of Kriya Yoga, which is to watch every breath, it is difficult to practice.

After the program was over and Baba left, some of our close friends asked us, "How did it feel to have a swami stay at your house?" This was not the first time a swami had visited us, however. We were fortunate to have hosted other swamis in the past. But with Baba, the experience was different. For Harinath and me, he very quickly seemed a beloved member of the family.

I remember my answer to their question. I said, "The only way I can describe it is, that it was like having a small child in the house. I was really struck by his child-like love, purity and freedom."

I can say one thing without any hesitation. I have heard about love of God and love for God from many monks before, but he was the first one who gave us some idea of what God's love is and how to love God. Perhaps it was his aura, or the way he was fully present, his selflessness, his magnetism, or the way he mingled with us closely as a part of the family, but for me, he brought God from the abstract to the concrete.

The Gita Lectures

When Baba visited us again we arranged a series of public lectures on the Bhagavad Gita at the temple in addition to the regular Kriya program. The Bhagavad Gita – literally translated as the Song of God, is a set of instructions on how to live one's life, given by Lord Krishna to his disciple, the Pandava prince Arjuna. Krishna delivers these explicit instructions on the battlefield and leaves nothing uncovered on how to live one's life both materially and spiritually.

There are three paths to salvation according to the Gita and each one, *karma yoga*, which is worship through work and duty without attachment to the results of action, *bhakti yoga*, which is worship through devotion, faith and surrender, and *jnana yoga*, worship through study, analysis and self knowledge, are all dealt with in an elaborate and complementary manner.

The Gita and its teachings were not new to me. I had a long history with the text, beginning with my college years in India.

✳ ✳ ✳ ✳ ✳ ✳ ✳ ✳ ✳ ✳ ✳ ✳ ✳ ✳ ✳ ✳ ✳ ✳ ✳

When I was still in college, I met a great spiritual master and teacher, Swami Chinmayananda. Swamiji was on a lecture tour conducting discourses on the Bhagavad Gita in the twin cities of Hyderabad and Secunderabad, and a discourse was scheduled at our school in Secunderabad. I had the chance to attend along with my mother. I was a member of the spellbound audience that Swamiji graced that day, with his enlightened, precise and scholarly lecture. He was a great orator. The audience included mostly the educated and elite of society. The talk was on the 13th chapter of the Bhagavad Gita.

At the time I did not have much of an introduction to the Gita except reciting chapters for contests. It was the first time I listened to an explanation of the verses. I was very impressed with the subject, as well as with his brilliant presentation and commentary. Although I did not understand the intricate text fully, I knew for the first time that Lord Krishna was not only a divine incarnation but was also the teacher of the Gita. Further, I learned that the Gita is a lesson on how to live a successful life and that it is the essence of the Vedas and the Upanishads and all holy Hindu scriptures. Swamiji's talk fueled my interest to study this scripture in depth.

Later, after my marriage, when we lived in Hyderabad in the early seventies after returning from our first stay in America, I was teaching at Women's College in the Chemistry Department. We were renting the first floor apartment in my coworker's building. Once a week, a Captain Rao would visit their apartment and hold *satsang* or group discussion on the Gita. One week we decided to go and join the *satsang* just to see what it was about. It was Captain Rao who first introduced me to the Gita Makarandam, a book in Telugu written by Swami Vidyaprakashananda Giri, a very brilliant and reputed swami. This swami had completed over one hundred *gita jnana yagnas* during his lifetime and was a great spiritual master. His commentary was so analytical and thorough, and the rendering so simple and clear, that I fell in love with the Gita. Until then, I had not clearly understood the role of Sri Krishna as the teacher of the greatest book on yoga. I was so excited that I shared my experience with my sister, Radha.

Radha and I seemed to have many common interests and some collective destiny too, including the same parents and the same in-laws. While still in medical school, she was married to my husband's younger brother Ravi, who was also a doctor. She was very interested in reading the Gita and would come home to do combined study with me. She was not good at reading Telugu, and so it was my duty to read and explain, and we also discussed the chapters together.

※ ※ ※ ※ ※ ※ ※ ※ ※ ※ ※ ※ ※ ※ ※ ※ ※ ※ ※

Gita in a New Light

Despite all of this history, Baba's Gita lectures marked the first time I was listening to the ancient familiar scripture in a totally new light. Baba started out by asking, "What is the Bhagavad Gita? Is it only a historic episode or a mythological story? Is it real or the poetic imagination of a saint? Is it a story, history or mystery, or all of these together? This depends on the depth of our understanding. If we can go beyond the characters and the drama or the historical and cultural aspect and we contemplate and meditate on the teaching, it becomes a mystery which still needs more study and more understanding."

The talks continued, and Baba enlightened the audience on how the Mahabharata war was not just an external war, but the inner battle that takes place constantly within each individual. Baba began to correlate each of the characters in the epic war with the inner instruments within each human body. It was fascinating, for example, to think of the weak and biased blind king Dhritarashtra as the blind mind. Gandhari, his queen, the wife of the mind, is material intelligence, which is equally blind, explained Baba, since she also blindfolded herself. Intelligence tends to be used in narrow ways without a broad understanding.

The Kauravas, he explained, were the multiple desires born of the blind mind and the equally blinded intellect. Baba reminded us that we have ten sense organs, five *jnanendriya,* or organs of knowledge, which include the eyes, nose, ears, tongue and skin, and five *karmendriya,* or organs of action, which include the mouth, hands, feet, genital organs and anus. The mind uses these ten organs to go in ten different directions, resulting in the hundred propensities, desires, thoughts, ambitions, expectations and dreams that human beings have. These are the Kauravas, the children of the mind, who are never satisfied and always fighting for more.

So where does meditation come in? Baba pointed out that meditation is the battle itself, where we have to fight with our lower qualities, destroy our distracted thoughts and go to thoughtlessness. Baba explained how each one of us is Arjuna, standing alone and confused in the battlefield. We have lost the divine kingdom for which we have to fight, but we are unwilling to, since we think of our many thoughts and desires as our close friends and kin. Lord Krishna represents the knowledge that is already within us, and only by surrendering to Krishna do we discover the knowledge that gives us the courage to fight and win.

The Bhagavad Gita (Chapter 13) speaks of *kshetra* (the field) and *kshetrajna* (the knower of the field). Baba explained that the human body and mind are similar to fields that have to be purified and cultivated through spiritual practice. The allegory of farming in spirituality is alluded to in scripture also.

Baba said his work as a spiritual teacher was not so different from that of a farmer. The farmer tills the ground, clears it of debris and stones, and makes the field ready for plantation. Once the seeds are sown, he irrigates the land with love and watches for sprouts. When there is a crop, he makes sure that the yield is not destroyed by insects.

A spiritual teacher is like the farmer who tills the ground of disciples' hearts, clears them of all negative thoughts, and sows the seed of spirituality. The initiation that a guru performs helps the seed to sprout. Just like the farmer continues in the face of pleasure or pain, the teacher continues to care for the student, trying to lead him Godward. In one of his talks, he said, "I am like a farmer. I have been farming and I will continue to farm whether the seed sprouts or not."

Baba's metaphorical interpretation in the light of Kriya Yoga illuminated many complex sections of the Gita, which I had not understood before. Well versed in Hindu scriptures, Baba taught with a deep compassion for humanity and love for God. It made me more inquisitive and triggered the urge to read more and go to a deeper level. The audience at the Cleveland temple sat spellbound through the talks, absorbing the unique method of his teaching and the vastness of his knowledge. I was so glad and did not want any of it to be forgotten. Fortunately, we recorded everything and I started transcribing the lectures at home.

At the time we first met Baba, my daughter Jyothi was living with us along with her son Nikhil, who was only ten years old. She had been through several years of physical and mental torment with her ex-husband, and we wanted her to meet with Baba and receive his blessings. Jyothi was completing her doctoral dissertation at the time. Going through an arranged marriage at 19 and getting divorced twelve years later, she had still managed during those turbulent years to finish her studies up to the Ph.D. level. Now a single mother trying to make a life for herself and her son, she would often become frustrated with the dissertation process and talk of giving up the program and focusing on her job. This saddened me, as I tended to blame myself, and our life decisions, for the situation she now found herself in.

I often wondered where our lives would have taken us if we never left our homeland. There is a steadiness that comes with staying in one place, a web of traditions, culture, family and values that buoys one up and removes uncertainty. Generations live and die, often in the ancestral home, each taking strength from the one before, each guiding the one after. Perhaps this was why the brahmins warned against leaving one's country behind, considering it a contamination. My husband's adventurous spirit and yearning ambition led us out of that cultural, spiritual, emotional and physical safety net, however, and took us across the *kala pani,* the dark waters that separated us from the western world and a very different value system.

* * * * * * * * * * * * * * * * * * * *

Crossing the Waters

In 1965, my husband had finished his Ph.D. in chemistry and started working as a Senior Research Chemist at the Regional Research Laboratories of Hyderabad. He also started applying for postdoctoral fellowships abroad and one fine day, came home with the news that he had been offered a fellowship at Northwestern University in Chicago. I applied for leave from my job teaching chemistry at Women's College and in 1967, in the month of April, we set out for Chicago with two of the children. We were advised to leave our youngest, Srinath, who was barely three months old and just beginning to smile at me in recognition, at home in the care of his grandparents. The idea was for me to complete my Ph.D. while I was abroad and our elders felt a young infant at that juncture would not only be a hindrance but would be neglected as well. He was raised very lovingly by both sets of grandparents in my absence, while I suffered intensely with guilt for having left him behind.

We landed in Chicago and spent three years at Northwestern University. Harinath was excited and passionate about his research work, arriving in the U.S. with two test tubes full of snake venom in his coat pocket and a child in each arm, eager to assist in the attempt to find a cure for Parkinson's disease.

Although I joined the Ph.D. program, it proved too difficult to accomplish with two small children and so I took a job as a

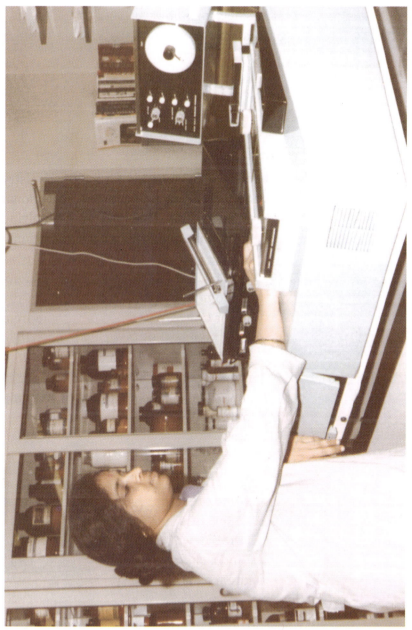

Conducting Research at Northwestern University

Harinath-Projects in Europe

biochemist instead, at the same university. The kids went to nursery and kindergarten in a private school. It was a chaotic time in history, and we sometimes feared for our safety, with Martin Luther King being assassinated and mass rioting in the streets of Chicago. We found some friends who would hold Gita classes once a month but lost interest when we found that the lunch took on more importance than the discussion itself. Life was quite hectic between work and family, and finally at the end of the three years, once my husband completed his postdoctoral research, we returned home.

We returned to India in 1970. I went back to teaching chemistry and Harinath got a job as Deputy Manager at Indian Detonators Limited –a big explosives company. We stayed in India for three years, and I attempted to make up for lost time and reconnect with my youngest son.

As fate would have it, we went back to the U.S. a second time. This time we went back with all three children as permanent residents with green cards. The children were adjusting as much as they could to all this moving back and forth, although it was not easy on them. They had to contend with being teased for their accents, learning to fit into a new culture, and an entirely different approach to academics.

We went back to Northwestern University, where Harinath had completed his research fellowship, and a year later he got a job as a manager in a chemical company downtown. He earned his M.B.A. degree from Kellog Business School, attending classes in the evenings, and eventually became the Business Development Manager of that company.

I continued at Northwestern University as a research associate. My job involved working in the medical oncology department, testing cancer drugs on laboratory mice. I was not happy with my role; it bothered me to inject the mice with disease, observe their growing tumors, and use experimental drugs to measure their effectiveness.

Unable to refuse the job, I struggled with my feelings and managed to push aside my misgivings in order to contribute to the family and pursue my career as a scientist. Finding myself in a research atmosphere, where all around me fellow scientists were working on larger animals, putting electrodes in cat brains, conducting experiments on baby monkeys and dogs, I justified my own work on rodents as not so cruel. I also convinced myself that the work I was doing served a larger purpose by contributing to a cure for a deadly disease.

It's interesting how we manage to justify our actions based on the environment we find ourselves in and the prevailing attitudes. Once caught up in the thrill of discovery and research, I pushed aside any ethical dilemmas and submerged myself in the science. I wrote several papers on my results, which were published in the National Institute of Health journal.

Still, I will always remember watching those little mice die within weeks of being injected with the cancer cells. It was something that I always regretted. When I spoke to Baba about it years later, he did not have any consolation for me. The acts we commit, whether good or bad carry their own consequences, he explained. Merely because we regret our actions or seek to outweigh them by good actions, we are not exempt from those consequences.

It is a sobering thought, that everything we do, whether in ignorance, whether with good intentions or otherwise, comes with a result. It shows the incredible importance of weighing every thought before it even translates into action, for it will inexorably and inevitably carry an inescapable consequence.

Another three years went by. By now, the children each had their own unique personalities. Jyothi was highly intelligent and a budding writer, winning prizes for her poetry in international competitions. She would write for hours in her journal, and read voraciously, painstakingly teaching herself to read Telugu just so she could devour the novels I had at home. Murali had decided very young that he would become a doctor when he grew up, and while shy, he always excelled academically. Soft-hearted and generous, he was first to offer up his savings for any worthy cause. Srinath was popular, very active and had many friends. Funny and mischievous, but not as focused on academics, he was mechanically inclined and incredibly curious, disassembling and reassembling everything he could get his hands on.

Over the next few years, we moved from suburb to suburb, Forest Park to Skokie to Glenview, gradually improving our economic status from renting apartments to buying a nice home, before my husband's job took us to Houston for a year. During this time, Mr. Varadarajan, the Managing Director of I.D.L. Chemicals Hyderabad, paid us a visit and offered Harinath a position as the Head of Research and Development in India.

The children were teenagers and we sent Jyothi, now fifteen and much too interested in boys, ahead to India to stay with her grandmother and to study there. A year later we took Mr. Varadarajan's offer and decided to move back to India as a family. Harinath was very excited about the opportunity to introduce solar energy in India with the help of a group from MIT and World Bank as part of his new assignment.

Life in India

We lived for a couple of years in a rented house, and then built a house of our own in Secunderabad. Once again, the children had to readjust, and now adolescents, they entered a phase of rebellion, experimentation and defiance. There was a lot of drama at home, and unprepared as I was for this phase, I did my best to handle it. Like most parents confronted by the next generation, I stumbled through, always with the best of intentions, but not always successfully. I had led a sheltered life as a child, and even as an adult, tended to follow the dictates of social norms and what was expected of me. The raw emotional displays, the passionate outbursts, the interest in the opposite sex that my daughter displayed as a teenager were both frightening and distasteful to me. Since she was the girl, I felt it was my particular responsibility to keep her safe until marriage.

Looking back, I could have been more understanding, been more of a friend and a confidante to her, but I shut her out and sought to beat, bully and threaten her into a more decorous mold. The boys got away with a lot of mischief with their friends, sometimes getting into deep trouble from which they would have to be rescued.

Fortunately for us, the deeply ingrained respect for education, the love and support of a large extended family, and the mantle of religion and tradition, all combined to keep our children on the proper path despite our ill preparedness, and they eventually emerged from their turbulent adolescence unscathed.

My daughter Jyothi, however, paid the price for my insecurities by being married off early to what seemed to be a respectable and educated young man, but who turned out to be dangerously imbalanced and both mentally and physically abusive. Unaware of his true nature, we came back to the United States with the young couple in tow, hoping that they too could settle here. I went back to work first at University of Illinois and then at University of Chicago as a research associate. Jyothi never told us what she was going through, attending school in Chicago and pursuing her Bachelor's, Master's and Doctoral degrees despite the torment she was undergoing at home. After suffering silently through 12 years of marriage and having a beautiful young son, she finally took steps to leave the marriage and file for divorce.

※ ※ ※ ※ ※ ※ ※ ※ ※ ※ ※ ※ ※ ※ ※ ※ ※ ※ ※

Jyothi's Initiation

As a result of her traumatic experiences in her marriage, Jyothi struggled with fear, stress, and anger, and reacted strongly to any form of criticism. She was unable to trust anyone and was very angry with the Divine Mother, whom she had worshipped devotedly from a young age, and whom she felt had abandoned her in her time of need. When we asked her to meet with Baba in the hope that he may help her, she initially refused and stayed at my sister Uma's house in nearby Ashtabula to avoid the whole visit.

Despite Jyothi's resistance and initial reluctance to attend the Kriya program at our home, we were somehow able to convince her to return during the program, at least on the last day before Baba left. Once she met Baba, everything changed. Not only did she find him fascinating, she wanted to be initiated immediately, and we had to take her the following weekend to the next program in Columbus, Ohio.

Here is what she wrote later about her meeting with Baba.

He was a small man, neither tall nor prepossessing. He lacked the physical stature that commanded my respect, and was dressed in an orange robe, with a black beard and unkempt hair. He was 37 years old, a former professor of economics who had taken sannyas or renounced the world, at the age of 35. I sat coldly before him; resistant, unwilling to show any respect to someone I did not know or care to know. My parents did not help by nudging me to ask questions. I told them bluntly that I had no questions and he submerged himself in a book. After sitting there for a while, I got up and went upstairs, where I stayed throughout the evening's meditation program.

It was after dinner, when he sat with a few loyal disciples gathered around him, that I ventured to re-enter the living room. I sat at a distance at first, but he looked up and said "I am very happy to see Jyothi Ma today."

I asked if I could ask him some questions. He agreed and so I moved closer and began my interrogation. To every question I asked, he had an answer. Unfazed by my aggressive, even rude comments, he answered me patiently and kindly. I sat talking with him till midnight. The next morning, I drove him to another disciple's house from where he would be leaving to the next town. As we sat and ate lunch there, we continued our conversation. As he left, he looked at me and said, "I will remember you. It has been less than 24 hours, but I am very happy."

I felt so drawn to him so quickly. I felt I could not bear to see him go. As he sat in the car, he told me, "Jyothi means light." I cherished those words as he drove away. I had no idea that I would be seeing him again in just a few days. My parents took me to Columbus to be initiated by him.

On July 13, 1997, I was given my first initiation into yoga by Swami Prajnanananda, who with his meditative powers, raised my consciousness, helped me perceive the blue light and the divine sound, and taking all my karmic burdens upon himself, endowed me with the purity, the energy and the love he had amassed through deep meditation. What a beautiful ceremony it is, with the lighting of the seven centers and the bonding of the guru and disciple in the journey toward the light. I shall never forget it as long as I live.

Teaching the Tiger

Jyothi's son Nikhil was also initiated into Kriya Yoga during one of Baba's visits. He was only ten, and one of the youngest disciples. Baba was staying with us at the time and the next day, as he passed Nikhil's room to come downstairs, he noticed something very interesting. Baba didn't mention anything to us during the day but at that evening's lecture, he shared a story with the audience. "Even the very young can benefit from yoga and meditation," he explained. "Take my youngest initiate. Not only is he practicing his technique with the greatest sincerity, he has already become a teacher. Today, I saw him teaching his stuffed tiger with great dedication how to perform a Kriya bow." The audience laughed with delight and I knew immediately that

Nikhil with Baba

he was referring to my grandson Nikhil. It was a story he continued to share in later programs. Nikhil was truly quite sincere in his meditation and the results were evident in later years.

Foundation Day in Florida

In August of 1997, the Florida Ashram moved from its rented quarters to a permanent place in Homestead. The Homestead property was very picturesque with many tropical flower and fruit gardens. September 22nd, the day of the equinox and a day of great yogic significance, was fixed as the Foundation Day of the ashram. We decided to attend the ceremony, and made a trip to the ashram along with some of our Cleveland group. Jyothi and Nikhil also came along with us.

The swamis were very loving and made sure our stay was comfortable. We were very happy to be participating in this historic moment. On the 22nd, we had a fire ceremony on the porch conducted by Baba and the other swamis with Gurudev seated on a chair and giving directions. We helped set up for the ceremony and made the *payasam* or rice pudding for *prasad*.

Meditating with Gurudev

Gurudev guided meditations during that time. It was a unique experience being guided by a realized Master. Being so closely attuned to the Divine, it was hard for him to stay on a lower plane, especially when meditating. Even as he was attempting to guide us through the process, he would involuntarily slip into a state of God consciousness and would leave us stuck and waiting in various postures for quite some time while he went into deep meditation. He was very solicitous of our progress however and repeatedly checked to see if we were all experiencing the full benefits of our meditation.

During one of the meditation sessions, Gurudev asked if everyone perceived the triple divine qualities of light, sound and vibration. Try as I might, I was not able to perceive the third quality. I raised my hand and said I was not feeling any vibration. He called me to come and sit near him and asked another swami to take care of guiding the group meditation. Such was his dedication that he proceeded to guide me individually, chanting the mantras of Mother Kali, touching each of the pulse points and making sure I was feeling the vibration. The touch of Gurudev was enough for me to immediately succeed in perceiving all three qualities, and I was deeply touched and inspired by that incident.

Despite his advanced stage, Gurudev was incredibly approachable and would talk to all of us. One morning after the meditation he said, "Harinath Baba, come and see me." All our family went in. Gurudev talked to all of us. Then he turned to our daughter Jyothi and asked if she wanted to get married again. She said she did not want to marry again after her bad experience. Gurudev assured her that it was okay if she did not remarry, but if she chose to, there was nothing wrong in it. He asked someone to bring a chocolate from the fridge and gave it to Nikhil.

We were all very happy with his blessings and came and told Baba about what happened. The next day during the evening meditation, Gurudev noticed that my husband was missing and asked where he was. Harinath had taken Nikhil to show him the beach. I was surprised how he remembered every one and noticed their absence even in that large group of people. We came back to Cleveland feeling very blessed.

Spreading the Word

The programs continued each year. Baba visited us sometimes twice a year if there was an additional retreat. Over the years, he was both a divine child that God had given us and also a mother, father, friend and guide. After the Cleveland program, there were also lectures in Fort Wayne, Indiana, Chicago, Illinois and Denver, Colorado. I went to most of these places and recorded the lectures with a mini cassette recorder in those days. Later the Kriya centers in each city began recording the lectures themselves. I requested the centers to mail the recorded tapes to me and transcribed all of them. By the summer of 1998, there were enough lectures transcribed to make a book. I tried to organize them into chapters with titles and subtitles, and soon I had a manuscript ready. My husband was a great support throughout and we spent many evenings together in front of the computer, revising the manuscript.

Whenever I looked at Baba while he was talking to others or giving a talk, I saw a light around him – a beautiful white light that sometimes extended to quite a distance. I wondered about it and asked him what it meant. "It could be you are concentrating or light is being revealed to you," was his answer. I felt it to be a great blessing. It would happen at the most unexpected moments.

Witnessing Samadhi

Baba allowed us to wash his feet very rarely and offer *arati* or vespers. These are experiences I cannot forget. He would close his eyes with eyebrows raised and suddenly he would seem to disappear, leaving only the physical shell behind. Once we would wash his feet, moving them became extremely difficult, since they would turn heavy as stone. He seemed so oblivious that sometimes we would have to call him several times before he opened his eyes again. We had not seen anyone in *samadhi* before and wondered if this was the *samadhi* state we had only heard or read about.

How beautiful it must be, I thought – he only has to raise his eyebrows and he is with God.

I remember another time when Baba was in Cincinnati for the Gurupurnima program. Quite a few disciples gathered at the home of Cincinnati center leader Yogacharya Bhadrayu Baba, and a celebration was arranged. The disciples requested the chance to wash his feet and Baba sat with eyes closed while a line of disciples offered flowers at his feet and bowed to him.

The process took quite some time and we noticed that Baba was completely without any movement throughout. Even after everyone was done, he still continued in that state sitting without moving, his face glowing with an unusual luster. After a few minutes, Bhadrayu Baba tried calling to him gently, "Baba, Baba," but there was no response. Then he gently touched him on his leg and realized by the feel of Baba's rigid body that he was in *samadhi*. After that touch, however, Baba came back to his surroundings and got up and left abruptly to his room, coming back in a few minutes after washing his face. Then the rest of the function went on. When I asked Baba about what happened, he said, "I was not there. I was gone."

Yet another time, we were in Ashtabula at my sister's house on a festival day. That morning Uma had requested a *pada puja,* or the chance to wash his feet. We washed his feet while Baba was in meditation, and it was once again really difficult to move his feet from the plate. As the years went by, the chance to witness this phenomenon became rarer as the crowds increased. The reverential ceremonies became more of a ritual and it seemed as though he was purposely keeping himself from ascending to that spiritual state in public.

Baba in Smadhi State

But there were a couple of occasions in India, when his *samadhi* state was apparent, and noticed by many. On one of Baba's birthdays in India at Balighai- I think it was the first time there was a big celebration and Baba was worshipped with 1008 lotus flowers, yielding to the request of the disciples. He sat among other monks on the dais and as the talks were given in his honor, followed by devotional singing, and lotus flowers were heaped around him, he went into *samadhi* again and had no knowledge as his garlands were adjusted. He stayed in that state for quite some time. When he came back to the present again, he went through the ceremony and later kept singing songs on Gurudev in an ecstasy for almost two hours.

One year, there was a group of doctors from the United States who came to serve in the Health Camps organized by the Prajnana Mission in neighboring villages, which Baba was to inaugurate that morning. Sometime after dawn, one of the monks at the Balighai ashram, Swami Samarpanananda, stumbled across Baba sitting in front of the Guru Mandir lost in *samadhi*. The news spread soon and a few of us, including a photographer on hand, were able to capture that moment.

The Midwest Centers

The Cleveland group grew over the years. Many new people were initiated and we had regular meditation classes weekly. Cleveland is within driving distance to many other locations in the Midwest, such as Cincinnati, Detroit, Fort Wayne and Chicago. During the next few years, new centers sprang up in Fort Wayne, Indiana, where Radha and Ravi lived, and also in Ashtabhula, Ohio, where Uma, my youngest sister, lived. We traveled with Baba to these places and helped in organizing and conducting the Kriya programs there. The centers started out in their homes for a few years and were shifted to other locations later. We also organized a program in Pittsburg with talks at the temple. There were initiations in Pittsburgh as well. Everywhere we went it was a great success, and his love and compassion won the hearts of all.

However busy he was, Baba always responded to sincere seekers and made time for his disciples. He was a teacher and a guide, who knew us as we really were, who knew our deepest flaws and continued to love us with a pure, all-encompassing and all-forgiving love. Only those who experience such love can truly appreciate his spiritual stature and the beauty of his wisdom.

Grace of the Guru

Baba knew how much people loved him and did his best to acknowledge each and every one. In those early days, before he became more inaccessible due to the large number of disciples and packed worldwide touring schedule, there were many precious memories gathered during the weekly programs he held across the country. At sumptuous lunches brought by dozens of ladies and served with love and affection, he would sit at the head of the table and lead us in prayer, never failing to compliment each person for the delicious food they brought. Each and every one felt special.

After lunch we would all sit around him and in response to the many questions we had, he would regale us with stories that held in their sweet simplicity, the perfect answer to our confusion. There were of course, as there always are when people gather, jealousies, possessiveness and ego conflicts, but he dealt with them all, teaching in his uniquely loving way. His discipline was never through enforcement, but through love, and through setting an example.

If he was staying at a disciple's home, however busy he might be, he came down from his room to see people in the family – the father leaving for the office, or the kids going off to school. When he was working on a book, he would sit in a place where the mother of the house would at least be able to see him, though he had perfect freedom to stay in his room and work.

I remember another time in Fort Wayne, Indiana. After three days of initiations and guided meditations, it was the last day of the program and the last guided meditation. Baba concluded by saying, "Thank you all and God bless you all" as he always does. No one in the audience looked like they had any intention of leaving. The silence was becoming a little awkward. Then with his charming smile, Baba said, "You all please close your eyes, I will sing a song and then we will finish." He sang, "*chalo man ganga yamuna teer*" - Oh mind, go to the banks of Ganga and Yamuna (the holy rivers of India). The mystic song has a beautiful inner meaning, with the rivers Ganga and Yamuna representing the inner spinal channels through which the mind merges into the Absolute in the fontanel. It goes on to describe the experience of the meditator seeing the different colors of divine light as shining jewels of the crown of Lord Krishna. Baba sang, stopping after each melodious verse to explain the meaning. The song was over. Still there was no movement in the audience. If anything, the song made it even harder to leave. Such is his aura and love.

The audience finally dispersed reluctantly and we had dinner. As much as possible, I bow to Baba's feet before going to bed. It was the last day in Fort Wayne and Radha and Ravi followed Baba into his room before I could do my *pranam*. They were talking to him about the horoscopes of their children. I thought it would be intrusive if I barged in, but I could not go to bed without bowing to him. I waited outside for some time, but they were having a lengthy conversation. I was miserable. I consoled myself thinking, "It is the last day here. Tomorrow Baba goes back with me to Cleveland," and went to my room.

I tried to sleep but could not. Finally I heard them leave. I debated for a few minutes whether I should go and bow to him. I went and bowed and talked to Baba about my meditation. What surprised me most was when he said, "As soon as they left, I came out looking for you, but you had gone to your room." So all that time when I was waiting, he knew I was waiting. It was the most memorable experience and one I will never forget.

Since then we had the honor of hosting Baba, as we lovingly called him, quite a few times. With each visit, many questions were answered and many doubts were dispelled - not necessarily through words. Baba gave many talks on the Bhagavad Gita, which drew large crowds who listened to his every word with rapt attention. At the end of his talks, many found it hard to leave the auditorium.

The more we listened, the more it became clear that it wasn't the words themselves which were so powerful, but the conviction and spirituality of the speaker that lay behind them. We had the good fortune of being close to him, compiling and transcribing his lectures and doing what we could for his mission. He became our loving guide and guru in every sense. God had finally given us a direction and we were grateful to be a part of this history.

Baba had become not just a part of the family, but the center of the family. What it was in him I do not know, but I knew he had become everything to me. My whole being was tuned to him and his words, and there was great pleasure in getting an email from him, even if it was only a few short lines of blessing.

For several years, I would email him each Thursday. I called it my Thursday *pranam*, with transcription questions, thoughts about scriptures I had read, or even issues that arose in daily life, and I would never fail to get a reply.

I wondered what the difference was between him and other monks whom I had met. There was an unpolluted simplicity, the purity of a child and a firm conviction and faith in whatever he said and did. Everything he did – his walk, his talk, his words, were filled with love. It must be the purity, energy and love he had gained through deep meditation, his relationship with his Master and communion with God. Each word that he spoke was as though measured and steeped in love. His voice was sweet and gentle, and though he acted simply, the wisdom and love were radiant in his face. He had so much compassion for one and all. It is said that even God thirsts for the love of devotees and God is love. It could be that we were all so thirsty for love, that when someone like Baba arrived, who gave love without any expectation, we tended to want more and more.

Although we look for happiness through many venues, the real bliss that we seek comes from love. We had never met anyone like Baba who had so much to offer. His love was not limited by place or time or occasion. He gave it freely, like a mother to her child, who loves him even when he is far off, even when he is sleeping unaware, even when he turns away from her in his childish pursuits.

Since that first meeting with the Guru, there has been only one priority in my life - to serve Baba and spread his teachings the best way I can. Suddenly, a clear and noble goal was before me, after years of working and taking care of the family.

3

REACHING THE
HIMALAYAN PEAKS

Baba loved India dearly and spoke often of how much he missed his three main sacred attractions: the Himalayas, the Ganga, and Jagannath temple in Puri.

He fondly recollected his visits to the Himalayas when he was very young. As he grew up, he felt a strong connection with the Himalayan Mountains and the holy river Ganges, which he suspected was an impression from past lives.

His first trip to the Himalayan foothills was as a schoolboy when he was 15. This was his first trip on his own outside of the state of Odisha, and it was an adventure. His travels took him to the metropolis of Delhi and on to Brindavan, the home and heartland of the *leela* of Lord Krishna. He visited the holy place of Rishikesh, home to many maths, ashrams, and saints, and continued to Dehradun and Mussoorie, all places where the mighty Ganges flows through unspoiled and lush Himalayan foothills.

On his first trip, he attended a training camp in Yoga and Vedanta. He was the youngest student. At the end of the course, there was a test. In that test, one candidate filled the entire answer sheet with the name of Rama and turned it in. The professor asked

Reaching the Himalayan Heights at Kedarnath

him why he would do such a thing. The student answered, "If the purpose of life is to know God, will this test help? I will get a certificate but will that help me to know God? It might only increase my ego. That is why I spent the two hours writing the name of God." That was an interesting experience for Baba. Baba returned to the Himalayas again and again. It was a place that his whole heart and soul adored.

He often said, "The Himalayas represents a spiritual father, a symbol of strength, magnanimity and determination. River Ganga is like the mother - loving, caring and ever purifying."

We had been to the foot of the Himalayas on our own before, as far as Rishikesh, but never into the mountains. When Baba was talking about the Himalayas, he described many holy places such as Badrinath, and Kedarnath, and the confluences of the holy rivers known as the *prayaga*, inspiring us so much that we decided to go to the Himalayas ourselves in June of 1998. By then, Baba had also planned to visit India and the Himalayas, even if for a short visit. When he mentioned his plans, we asked if we could join him in India at Rishikesh. By God's grace, everything came together.

Meeting at Rishikesh

The four of us, Harinath, Jyothi, our grandson Nikhil, and I, traveled to India and reached Rishikesh and the Dayananda Ashram, where we planned to stay before setting out for the Himalayas.

Baba left for India a few days before us, and after visiting Mathura and Brindavan, he met us at Rishikesh as planned. Baba had arrived that morning along with Swami Swarupananda and was at Dayananda ashram. It was also our first meeting with

Swarupananda, who came to us and introduced himself, and led us to the room where Baba was.

Baba said he was so thrilled with his recent visit to Mathura and Brindavan that he had rolled in the sacred dust, the playground of Krishna's childhood pranks. Baba loved Krishna so much that when he talked about the exploits of Krishna, it seemed as though the child Krishna had appeared before us in Rishikesh.

Rishikesh, which literally means the locks of the sages, is a reference to location and history. The city is situated in the foothills of the Himalayas, where countless saints and sages live and meditate. This is where the Ganga emerges from the mountains and flows across the northern plains. The city is filled with several temples that line the banks of the Ganga, with the holy city of Haridwar just one hour to the south.

※ ※ ※ ※ ※ ※ ※ ※ ※ ※ ※ ※ ※ ※ ※ ※ ※ ※

This was not the first time that I had visited Rishikesh. When I was a young girl, my father worked in the Railways, so we had free rail passes and travelled quite often to places of pilgrimage. On one such trip to Delhi, Haridwar and Rishikesh, we visited the Divine Life Society, the ashram of Swami Sivananda.

Sivananda Ashram

Swami Sivananda was a physician who, in his divine quest for truth, became a realized master and decided to be a spiritual doctor instead of a medical doctor. He was the founder of the Divine Life Society, which has become one of the most reputed spiritual organizations of India and is still a landmark in the Rishikesh area.

My mother knew of Swamiji and his teachings, and shared some of her knowledge with me. It was nice to visit the ashram back then and we bought a few books. I must have been thirteen at the time. Even then, I was impressed with the clear, simple and practical instructions of this great spiritually realized master, and I did use those instructions during the beginning of my *sadhana*.

Dayananda Ashram

The founder of the Dayananda Ashram, Swami Dayananda Saraswati, is a great scholar and teacher of Vedanta. We were fortunate to have known him closely.

He established traditional teaching centers under the name of Arsha Vidya Gurukulam. Swamiji's central mission was the teaching of the Upanishads. He gave hundreds of discourses and wrote numerous books of great wisdom. In the 1980's when Swamiji came to the United States to find a suitable place to establish an ashram, he stopped at Fort Wayne, Indiana, to visit Ravi and Radha. We were living in Chicago at the time and he paid us a visit as well.

His mission was successful and Arsha Vidya Gurukulam in Saylorsburg, Pennsylvania was established in 1986. He also established another ashram with the same name in Coimbattore, India, in 1990. We visited him in Saylorsburg when the ashram was being constructed and also attended programs there later. Swamiji is an internationally recognized teacher, who elaborates on the *vedantic* truths with great love and compassion, along with a unique sense of humor.

The Rishikesh Ashram was established by him in 1960. Regular residential courses based on the Gita and Upanishads are conducted at this ashram by Swamiji and his disciples.

✳ ✳ ✳ ✳ ✳ ✳ ✳ ✳ ✳ ✳ ✳ ✳ ✳ ✳ ✳ ✳ ✳ ✳ ✳

Love of the Sacred Ganga

Dayananda Ashram is situated right on the banks of the holy Ganges and one can just walk down a few steps to the river.

As we stared in awe at the rushing waters of the sacred river, Baba shared with us that even as a child he had heard many stories of Ganga, which in Hinduism, is not regarded as an inanimate river, but as the living presence of the Divine Mother herself. It is said Mother Ganga falls from a lock of hair on Lord Siva's head and her descent to earth is to purify and love all those who come to bathe in her waters.

Baba said he was about fourteen years old when he had his first *darshan* of Ganga. It was at Haridwar in the month of August. When he entered the cool waters of Ganga, he did not want to come out. Never mind the coolness of the waters, he knew deep inside that he was in the lap of his own Divine Mother and felt that she was singing to him. He said he came out reluctantly with tears in his eyes, praying for another chance to be back.

That afternoon, we took a bath in the Ganga, which was so exhilarating and refreshing that my daughter Jyothi summed up both the physical and spiritual experience in the following words:

Ganga is considered a great purifier loved, revered, and extoled by poets, saints and sages through the ages. There is an immense power in her, which rushes through the body, lighting the hidden fire of divinity, washing away the accumulated dirt and dust of worldly desire and struggle, and strengthening the bond between the individual and universal soul.

If washing away sin means washing away the anger, vanity and confusion of the human mind, if removing sorrow is to remove the paltry desires, which torment our earthly existence, then yes Ganga does indeed do this. Immersed in her throbbing and pulsating current, the soul is at last free of all material burdens and joy, sorrow, pain and pleasure all disappear in the ecstatic state of pure bliss. No wonder then that through the ages she has been the haven for saints and sinners alike, for in those moments one gains the freedom which whole lifetimes cannot achieve.

She cannot give us redemption, but she can show us what it is like. She is God's handmaiden, sent to urge us towards Him, washing His lotus feet, she gives us a taste of what bliss can be and helps us remember who we are. It is a pity that most of us emerge from the Ganga only to roll again in our bad past habits and weaknesses, desires and wants, gradually forgetting what it is she has given us - a priceless gift which we need to cherish and nourish in order for it to bloom in us.

From Rishikesh, we proceeded on our trip to Kedarnath and Badrinath, with Baba as our guide. Once on the mountain peaks of the majestic Himalayas, it was a heavenly experience. Mother

Ganga accompanied us throughout, rushing along in the valleys by the side of the entire stretch of winding mountain roads. It was like a place ethereal, which did not belong to any earthly plane or region. Indeed, one had to question, "Is this earth or heaven or some other plane?" Many times we had to remind ourselves where we were. Many stories from mythology came to mind. Even to this day, people believe that many celestial beings, saints and sages roam the Himalayas in their subtle bodies, helping those who are really in search of God.

Kedarnath

The trip to Kedarnath was not easy. It was our first experience of such a journey. We traveled on mules for nearly two hours along steep mountain curves with no barriers to prevent us from tumbling into the deep gorge below. It was a little frightening. Baba refused to ride the mules, insisting on walking up the entire mountain.

When we finally reached the 13,000 ft. summit, the views were spectacular. The temple stood in ancient splendor before us. The Kedarnath shrine is surrounded by snow-covered mountains and grassy meadows. Near Kedarnath is the source of the river Mandakini that joins river Alakananda at Rudraprayag. Behind the temple is the high peak that can be seen from great distances. At the entrance of the temple is the statue of Nandi, the divine bull of Siva. The Siva Lingam in the temple is of an unusual pyramidal form.

The temple would be closing at noon and by the time we reached the summit, it was getting close to that time. We joined the *darshan* lines and waited for Baba to show up. As we were about to step into the main temple, Baba appeared and was ushered in from a side door. We were able to go in together for the *darshan* of Lord Kedarnath.

Afterwards we visited the *samadhi* place of Adi Shankara, which was close to the temple. Adi Shankara is believed to be the incarnation of Lord Siva himself, who incarnated to save *sanatana dharma*, the Eternal Religion of India, popularly and mistakenly reduced to Hinduism. He was a child prodigy who accepted *sannyasa* at the age of eight, and wrote commentaries on all the major works of Advaita Vedanta. He lived in universal consciousness, but at the same time had great compassion for humanity. He worked toward helping each human being realize that God is within, in others, and everywhere.

Baba loved Shankara and referred to and quoted Shankara so much in his talks, that I considered him to be a Shankara of this modern age. Baba spent some time at the *samadhi* silently meditating. Visiting that sacred spot with Baba was a memorable experience.

Badrinath

After experiencing the wonders of Kedarnath, we proceeded to Badrinath. If Kedarnath is dedicated to Lord Siva, then Badrinath is considered the earthly abode of Lord Vishnu. It is a place where Nara and Narayana, man and God, are believed to have performed penance in ancient times, and is therefore a place of great spiritual significance. We had the *darshan* of the beautiful idol of Lord Badrinath. The priest in the temple garlanded Baba with the *tulasi* garland from the idol of Badrinath.

We came out and circled the temple. Adi Shankara's presence was still tangible here as well. A lifelike statue of Sri Shankara teaching his four chief disciples adorned the temple premises.

We sat there and recited *vishnu sahasranama*, the 1000 names of Lord Vishnu.

Our treks of the past few days reminded me of *guru govinda darshana*. The guru is the one who leads you to God. Just as we needed a guide to lead us on the treacherous path up the mountains to the temples, we needed a guide to protect us on the slippery spiritual path, which the scriptures describe as walking on the edge of a sharp razor. The spiritual path becomes easier when you have a guide, who has himself traveled it and is familiar with all its twists and turns. We sat around Baba, who was silent. Lord Dakshinamurthy observed silence when disciples approached, and yet his silence removed all doubts. I remembered reading somewhere that the highest form of grace is silence and it is also the highest spiritual instruction. If the guru is silent, the seeker's mind gets purified on its own. Silence is the utmost eloquence. It transcends speech and thought. Just sitting near him in that holy atmosphere was at once purifying and elevating.

From Badrinath, we started our return journey. When we stopped in the evenings, sometimes in places on the banks of the Ganga, we bathed in the cold, refreshing water of the greatest purifier. Sometimes Baba would tell us stories from mythology. He told us about the descent of Ganga to the earth and how Bhagiratha performed penance for many years to bring her down to earth to release his forefathers from a curse and liberate them. The week with our guru in the Himalayas and with Mother Ganga was hectic, but beautiful beyond description.

Baba had a clear vision of his future activities and the building up of an ashram in India. He often talked about other ashrams, the spiritual and charitable activities they were undertaking, and how we should also implement them. Even at that time, he had the vision of starting a school for children introducing spiritual curriculum, and to do something for the sick and poor. His thoughts and presence were so inspiring that we as a family then were totally involved in whatever he wanted to do, and decided to use what little skills we had to support his work. It was a great feeling to be associated with his lofty vision and ideals, which as individuals we could not think of. He knew his mission and we were fortunate to be a part of it.

Printing the Gita Discourses

When we set out for the Himalaya trip, I also took the draft of the transcribed Gita lectures with us. I was hoping I could ask Baba to look it over and get his permission to print the book while I was in Hyderabad. When I presented it to him during our trip to the Himalayas, he graciously consented to read the draft and approved it.

When I was in Hyderabad, I showed it to my father, who was so pleased and excited about his daughter doing such good work. I also requested that he read the draft and write a foreword to the book. He felt it was a great honor. I remember exactly what Father said about this golden opportunity I had with Baba. "In the world there are many scholars much more knowledgeable than us, but the opportunity to do such work is a rare privilege, and that is possible only with the grace of God."

Father helped me contact a press and I spent quite a few evenings there to get the book printed. I came back with 1500 copies of the book. Soon after that, there was a program in Cleveland and Baba was there. I had great pleasure in presenting the book to him and getting his blessings. When he was in Miami, Baba said he showed the book to Gurudev, who read the book from beginning to end, and was very happy. This was the beginning of the many books that Baba's teachings produced. The Gita lectures continued and so did my transcribing and the work resulted in a second volume of discourses that was published by Prajnana Mission in the year 2000.

During Baba's visits, we learned about Odisha where he was from, about Cuttack and the ashram he had at Jagatpur, and how much he wanted to visit Odisha again. He also talked about Swami Brahmananda Giri and Swami Shuddhananda Giri, whom he had left in charge and whom he missed very much.

On my next visit to India, I wanted to meet these monks. I contacted Cuttack and learned that Swami Brahmananda and Swami Shuddhananda were on a program tour during the time I was visiting and would be in the port city of Vishakhapatnam on certain dates. I had not visited the city before and had wanted to for some time. We had friends there and so I decided to meet the monks in Vishakhapatnam.

Simhachala Temple

Taking my co-sister Sujata with me, I went to Vishakhapatnam and visited our friends. I also wanted to visit Simhachalam which was nearby – to have the *darshan* of Lord Narasimha at the famous temple. My mother had often told me about Vishakhapatnam, where she went to college for some time, and of the Narasimha temple she had visited as a student.

When we contacted the Kriya program organizer, he gave us the details of the program and also mentioned that the swamis would visit the Simhachala temple the next day.

Simhachala literally means the hill of the lion and gets its name from the hill on which the temple of Lord Narasimha – the Man Lion sits. We planned on visiting the temple the next day,

Meeting the Monks at Simhachalam

happy that we could meet the swamis in such a sacred location. The way up to the temple runs through terraced fields of pineapple, mango and jackfruit trees. There are a thousand steps that lead up to the temple for those who choose to walk, with trees planted on either side to afford them shade, but we took the car all the way up.

Once we entered the temple, I was surprised to see that the idol in the sanctum sanctorum, the shape of which we could not clearly see, was completely covered in sandalwood paste. We were told that it was the custom there to worship the Lord this way without exposing his image. Only once a year, on the third day in the month of May, the sandalwood paste can be removed and his real form worshipped. These instructions were supposedly handed down by an *akashavani,* a voice from the heavens, to a king who rebuilt the temple.

Simhachala is considered to be the actual spot where Prahlada was rescued from his evil father Hiranyakashipu by Lord Vishnu, in the form of Narasimha. Prahlada's father Hiranyakashipu hated Lord Vishnu because he killed his evil brother Hiranyaksha. His son Prahlada however, happened to be a staunch devotee of the same Lord Vishnu. Unable to change his son's mind and furious at him for continuing to have faith in his enemy, Hiranyakashipu attempts to put his own son to death.

At first he tries having him thrown in the ocean to drown. When that doesn't work, he has him pushed from a high mountain top. Finally he tries to have him trampled by elephants. When none of these methods work, he goes into a rage, asking Prahlada to show him his Lord that he has such faith in. Prahlada replies, "He is everywhere."

Furious, Hiranyakashipu points to a pillar and kicks it demanding, "Is he here as well?" At that very moment, Lord Vishnu emerges from the pillar in the form of Narasimha, who is half man and half lion. Since Hiranyakashipu has a boon that prevents him from being killed by either man or beast, Lord Narasimha is neither one nor the other, but a combination of both. Narasimha lifts Hiranyakashipu into his lap because the boon also states that he cannot be killed either on land or in the sky. Narasimha then tears Hiranyakashipu from limb to limb, killing him.

Baba once explained that the Lord can take one of two manifestations. Either He can appear as Rama, Krishna, Jesus or Buddha, or any other incarnation, being born, going from childhood to manhood and then spreading the word of God through his actions or message, or He can take on a form with the immediate purpose of relieving His disciples from hardship. Lord Narasimha, he explained, was just such a manifestation, intended to provide instant relief from prolonged misery.

Meeting the Monks

It was close to noon and the temple was about to close for lunch. We were anxiously waiting for the swamis and just at the moment, we saw two orange-clad holy men walking in with a few disciples. We waited outside for them to emerge, and then I introduced myself to Swami Brahmananda and Swami Shuddhananda, eager to learn more about them.

Swami Brahmananda was a senior monk and a long-time disciple of Paramahamsa Hariharananda. Swamiji was with the education department of the State of Odisha in his premonastic life. Even while active in the world, he led a life of celibacy and strict spiritual discipline. A humble monk of profound wisdom, he was at the time in charge of the Jagatpur Ashram near Cuttack, Odisha. He also toured the many Kriya centers in India, spreading the message of Kriya Yoga.

Swami Suddhananda was a young, dynamic monk, also a native of Odisha and a disciple of Paramahamsa Hariharananda. Formerly an engineer by profession, he had an intense desire for spiritual knowledge from his childhood and joined the monastic order at a very early age.

If Swami Brahmananada was Baba's right hand, then Suddhananda was his left, each doing their best to support him in all his endeavors and managing the India ashrams in his absence. I was thrilled to meet these two beautiful monks and share stories of our experiences with Baba. After having met them, I decided to go to the program to attend the meditation the next day. It was nice to see how much they loved Baba and how anxiously they were awaiting his return. I came back home after the trip, just in time for the Midwest retreat.

4

THE BIRTH OF A PARAMAHAMSA

In 1998, Ohio was chosen to have the first Midwest Kriya Retreat and our Kriya group from the Cleveland area had to organize it. It was a new experience but also a lot of fun. The retreat site was beautifully situated on acres of lush farmland lined with trees, and nestled beside a lake. It was a four-day retreat, and those who attended felt truly blessed. The theme for the retreat was yoga as a path to spirituality. There were two discourses every day and Baba spoke on many interesting and useful topics, including the different states of mind, yoga in daily life, balancing work, family, and spiritual life, attaining emotional balance, and the true guru disciple relationship.

Baba explained in detail about the mind, all the obstacles it creates on the path, and how to overcome them. It was interesting to hear that there were five states of the human mind.

1. The first state is one of dullness, where the mind is lethargic and unfocused.

2. The second state is one of restlessness, where the mind cannot focus on any particular thing and jumps from one thought to another.

Paramahamsa Prajnanananda

3. The third state is one of limited concentration, where the mind is wholly absorbed in one or the other sensory pleasure: food, drink, lust, etc.

4. The fourth state is one of concentration on one's goals.

5. The fifth and final state is one of complete control, where the mind is no longer in charge, but is used to serve a higher purpose.

As Baba described each of the states of mind, I reflected on my own mind. Although I found myself in the fourth state most of the time, deeply focused on what I had to accomplish, Baba had warned that even this state of concentration could have some pitfalls. He explained that if the mind in such a state chose to focus on the negative, then it could obsess on the negative to the exclusion of everything else. I knew I had this problem sometimes when my mind would get absorbed with trivial incidents and obsess over what someone said or what someone did, wasting a lot of time. Baba's words made me realize the importance not only of concentration, but of being able to focus on the right things. "Be careful of what you think and what you wish" were his words. I tried to take those words to heart from that day onward.

During the retreat, Baba also guided three meditations each day. With love and encouragement, Baba inspired us to have more discipline and more good habits and more compassion. It was a precious experience to be in the presence of one who loved us like a mother, disciplined us like a father, and guided us with care and understanding. We experienced a happy feeling of surrender, which is the basis for a true guru disciple relationship.

After the Ohio retreat, I started transcribing the recordings of the retreat lectures. Transcribing and compiling them resulted in a nice book and we decided to call it *Yoga: Pathway to the Divine*. The draft was sent to Baba who made the corrections, and the manuscript was soon ready for printing. Baba gave us the freedom to choose the cover and we chose a picture of him sitting under a tree beside a stream. It was a beautiful cover for a beautiful book.

The Birth of a Paramahamsa

During conversations we once asked Baba about his date of birth. He would not answer. Then we kept guessing month by month till we came to August, when he kept quiet. Then I went day by day and when we came to the 10th, he did not say anything again. That's how we discovered that his date of birth was August 10th. We requested that he be in our midst on that day and he said he would see. Fortunately, it was close to the Ohio retreat time, and he would still be within the state.

We had moved to a new house in Hudson, Ohio, and we named our house Prajnana Nilayam in Baba's honor. We invited all the Kriyavans in Cleveland and also some close disciples from Detroit and Cincinnati for the birthday celebration on the evening of August 10th. On the 9th of August, Baba was concluding a program in Columbus, Ohio. We drove to Columbus that day to attend the program and after dinner drove him back to Hudson, Ohio. By the time we reached home, it was midnight.

Traveling with Baba in the car was a wonderful experience. Baba would talk with great love about Odisha and the Jagannath Temple, or would be singing songs in his sweet melodious voice. Even though he was tired, he would talk to give us his company, and most of the time we learned so much from these seemingly casual conversations.

According to Hinduism, a guru represents the first Guru, Lord Siva. My husband performed the *abhisheka*, a ritualistic sacred bath, as part of his worship of Siva every morning. We had the wish to perform the *abhisheka* for our guru on his birthday, a rare opportunity that God had provided us. Still, we were a little hesitant to ask. We got up early as usual, and finished our morning worship and had everything ready for Baba's bath, along with the new clothes that I had brought for him from my last trip to India. We waited for the door to Baba's room to open. Then my husband made the request. I have the feeling that Baba weighs the earnestness with which any request is made before he agrees to it. Looking at my husband and knowing his devotion to Siva, he consented to the *abhisheka*. We had some Ganga water that we mixed in the tap water and we ceremoniously poured water over his head, reciting the *rudram,* a sacred hymn dedicated to Lord Siva.

We were so excited and happy to be given this opportunity to worship Lord Siva in Baba's form. Having finished his bath, Baba wore his new clothes and looked radiant. We also asked him if we could perform a short fire ceremony to propitiate the nine planets and Lord Siva for blessings on his birthday, to which he graciously agreed. We started the fire ceremony in Baba's presence. The telephone rang but we did not answer it. We could hear a recording but it was not clear. After we concluded the ceremony, we listened to the recorded message. It was the voice of Gurudev Paramahamsa Hariharananda calling from Vienna!!!. It was a birthday greeting. "Today is the most auspicious day. It is the birthday of Paramahamsa Prajnanananda. Today I confer all my blessings on you as Paramahamsa."

As we listened to the message, the phone rang again and Baba picked up the receiver. It was Gurudev calling back to say, "From today I give you the title of Paramahamsa. So you are no more Swami Prajnanananda, from today you are Paramahamsa Prajnanananda."

Gurudev Hariharanandaji conferred the title of Paramahamsa, the highest title reserved for monks, who attain the summit of realization, who are inspired and divine teachers, guides and saints, on his chosen disciple and successor, our beloved Baba Prajnanananda, on that August 10, 1998.

At 7 p.m. that evening, the brightly decorated hall in our home was filled with people who had come from as far away as Rochester and Detroit, and were waiting for Baba to join them. The evening began with a short prayer by Baba. There followed a beautiful session of devotional songs, sung melodiously and with great ardor by all the devotees. After the songs, my husband played the recorded message of Gurudev Hariharananda announcing Baba's new title of Paramahamsa. There was a burst of spontaneous applause, from people who were overjoyed to hear the voice of Gurudev recorded that morning, conferring the title. It was a day of double blessing.

Finally, as the high point of the evening, the new Paramahamsa gave his birthday message of love, extoling the virtues of parents, human and divine, and the process of growth which takes place under the loving guidance of the guru, who is both mother and father in the miracle of one's spiritual birth. He bowed finally to his own guru and to all the gurus before him and to those who were present, reminding us in his own eloquent way, of the divinity within us all. He ended by leading us in a song of his own composition.

Father of all, my Mother of all
I am Thy child, please listen to my call.
I am Thy child, I cry for Thee
Come to me, God come to me.

Afterward, I offered *arati* to Baba and the group sang along. Then came the chance for each of us to receive our guru's blessings. This was followed by dinner, a feast prepared by many devoted hearts and hands, and a delicious assortment of desserts served personally by the guru's loving hands. To this day we are grateful to God and gurus to be present at that moment in history when a Paramahamsa was born. It was a beautiful evening spent acknowledging the auspicious moment when Baba's life began and the endless spiritual riches that life has conferred upon our own.

Baba had now joined the august ranks of saints like Paramahamsa Yogananda, Paramahamsa Ramakrishna, and his own master Paramahamsa Hariharananada as one of the bright stars in the spiritual firmament. His birthday celebration was merely an expression of the love and gratitude we all feel for everything he has done for our own progress and enlightenment.

Only a worthy Master can produce a worthy disciple. Gurudev had blessed the world with this special disciple, a true reflection of his Master to continue his mission. Like Ramakrishna Paramahamsa who gave the world Vivekananda, Gurudev gave us Paramahamsa Prajnanananda. Gurudev had said, "He is not different from me. I have given him everything."

Immortalizing the Kriya Lineage

From a very young age, Baba was thirsty for knowledge and was an avid reader. Baba later remarked that books became his best friends and he never went anywhere without carrying a book to read. It was not easy to get books, especially spiritual books, while growing up in a village. As a teenager, he found a book entitled, *How to Cultivate Values and Eradicate Vices* by Swami Sivananda. It included an exhaustive list of virtues and vices, major and minor, for each person to cultivate or eradicate in life. He would go through those lists checking to see his own strengths and weaknesses.

We are all soldiers fighting the battle of life, he reasoned, and when a soldier knows the strength and weakness of the enemy, he can fight better. Our vices are our enemies and we have to sacrifice our negative qualities. He wondered how sometimes we do not want to give up our vices thinking we cannot survive without them. As he was later to discover in the Bhagavad Gita, in the battlefield of life, our enemies are within, and self-mastery is akin to victory. As Lord Krishna says to his student Arjuna, "Oneself is one's own friend and oneself is one's own enemy." [Gita, verse 5, Chapter 6]

When he went on to his undergraduate studies in Cuttack, there was a bookshop near the college from where he regularly borrowed spiritual books. He was on the best terms with most of the booksellers in the city, and they would let him borrow whichever books he wanted to read. He would handle every book with extreme care, not damaging the pages, and would return them intact. This was a great privilege, as a student's budget doesn't stretch too far. Even in his adult years, he could not sleep unless he had a book by his pillow.

In the year 1998, Baba was working on many books. One day he asked if I was interested in editing some books. He offered to send me the manuscripts so I could work on them. I was more than happy to be able to do it. The first manuscript we received was the life of Sri Lahiri Mahashaya, a handwritten manuscript. We worked on it together as a whole family. Harinath would be typing, I would do the preliminary editing, and Jyothi would give the final touches. If we had any doubts or questions, we could contact Baba through email or telephone and Baba was always prompt in answering.

The second manuscript he sent was the biography of Swami Shriyukteshwar. It was a wonderful experience doing this work in close association with Baba and it was also our good fortune to study the lives of the great Kriya masters of our lineage, of whom we knew very little.

Then came the biography of Gurudev himself. In this context, I remember a conversation with Gurudev on one of our visits to Miami. Sitting near him in his room once, I said to Gurudev, "Gurudev, I could come and stay in the ashram for some time. I would like to write about your life if you could tell me some incidents." Gurudev smiled and replied, "There is no need. Prajnanananda has it all in his brain in black and white, I hope." Little did I know at that time that these pages of Gurudev's biography would be going through our hands. Baba would send material as recorded cassettes and we worked in close collaboration with fellow Kriyavans Pratima and Srinidhi of Denver. Pratima would transcribe the tapes and after Srinidhi's preliminary corrections, the transcripts would come to us along with the cassettes. Then we would do more editing and send the transcripts to Baba for corrections. It was a great pleasure to listen to the recordings of Baba's sweet gentle voice speaking and you felt like he was there next to you giving dictation.

We just kept working during those times till the work was done, sometimes early in the morning and sometimes late at night. It was great teamwork, and Baba kept us inspired. For the cover of this book on Gurudev, we decided to use a photograph of a waterfall that we had taken during our Himalayan trip and the title was to be *River of Compassion* in consultation with Baba.

Celebrating Gurudev's Birthday

Baba sent the books for printing to India so they would be ready before Gurudev's birthday on May 27, 1999. Before that time, we wanted to record some of Baba's devotional songs during one of his visits. Luckily, we had some really good musicians and instrumentalists among the disciples of Cleveland. We asked Baba's permission to record and he agreed. He sang for a few hours nonstop.

We were all amateurs. Baba directed the orchestra, telling them when to stop and when to play, and with his guidance, we were able to record two 90-minute cassettes. We did the recording in the basement of our house in Hudson. We also had help from our friends in printing labels for the cassettes. It was almost like a small cottage industry. We had the labels on the cassettes and they looked really good.

For Gurudev's birthday that year, we decided to send him a birthday card and Baba's cassettes of devotional songs. Jyothi had written a beautiful tribute called "The Divine Gardener" and we sent the scroll and the cassettes to Baba to be presented to Gurudev.

Baba later told us how pleased Gurudev was with the books, the poem and the cassettes, and how he listened to the songs all day and sang along with them. We felt really blessed to have played a part in creating them. Jyothi's framed poem is still in the Homestead ashram to this day.

More Books and Discourses

Baba also wrote *My Time with the Master* as a sequel to *River of Compassion*. While the first book was more of a biography of Gurudev, in the second book, Baba shares his private memories of his life under the direction of his great master and the training he received.

The publishing work continued, now with additional help. By now Prajna Publications was formed in Vienna and disciples from the Vienna ashram were actively involved. The publications were of high quality and resulted in some very attractive books.

The Universe Within

The second Ohio retreat, held in 1999, was even more interesting than the first, and Baba's talks were extremely enlightening. He described how the five elements of nature, the earth, water, fire, air and sky, constitute the outer physical universe, and how the same elements also constitute the inner universe. The body, mind and the *chakras* were dealt with in detail. It was interesting to study the different elements and their characteristics. The lectures from this second retreat resulted in the book, *The Universe Within*.

Krishna Katha and *Rama Katha*

During a ten-day retreat at the Tattendorf Ashram in Vienna, Baba first started talking about the life of Krishna and these talks continued later at other places. This retreat followed Baba's birthday on August 10th, which was celebrated that year in Vienna.

Baba's love for Krishna was so intense and he was so absorbed in describing the childhood pranks of Krishna, that to me he looked like the child Krishna when he was speaking about him. Baba had such a wonderful way of making a story interesting, he would play the characters in the story.

The description of Krishna's pranks were the best I had ever heard. "The Gopis were very fond of Krishna. When they invited him to their houses Krishna would ask, "What will you give me? I want butter and sugar candy." The Gopis would ask, "How much?" Stretching his little hands wide apart, Krishna would say, "This much." Baba would look just like the child Krishna, stretching his hands wide apart. "Can you eat so much?" asked the Gopi. "I will feed all my friends and also the monkeys," would be Krishna's reply.

In this sweet way, Baba poured out the nectar of *Krishna Katha*, the story of Krishna's life, unfolding the lessons to be learned from every incident related to the birth and divine activities of Krishna.

When you listen to these stories of people who loved and lived in God, it inspires you and ignites the flame of love in you. Just as Krishna moved the people from the village of Gokula to the village of Brindavan, our compassionate Baba transported his spellbound audience from Gokula (the place of senses) to Brindavan (the garden of love) through his love and wisdom. This is where the seeds were sown for my compiling the book *Krishna Katha*. We were able to release the book in time for Baba's next birthday.

The book *Rama Katha*, on Lord Rama, was a result of a weeklong lecture program in Kansas ending with Lord Rama's birthday, which that year was on the 29th of April, which also happened to be our wedding anniversary.

When I wrote to Baba about it before he came to the program, he said "Good, we will do a *havan* for Sri Rama on that day." We performed a fire ceremony at home on the 29th of April in Baba's presence.

The lectures on Rama that week were truly inspiring. As Baba sat humming the song of Tulasi Das *"tumaku chalata Ramachandra"* before each lecture, I could visualize the little Rama taking his first steps with his anklets making musical sounds to the delight of his mother Kausalya. I got to work right away compiling his lectures. I had hoped to release the book on Baba's birthday on August 10th, like I did the *Krishna Katha* before, but Baba decided to release it for Gurudev's birthday in May. After that I was silent, and thought to myself, I have dedicated it to Baba in my heart, let him do as he pleases.

Bhaja Govindam and *Dasha Shloki*

Since then I completed one compilation of his work every year as a birthday dedication –whether or not it was released was immaterial to me. That is how I finished the *Kaivalyopanishad*. I even presented the draft on August 10th in Vienna. After that I compiled the *Bhaja Govindam* and the *Dasha Shloki* and presented him the drafts when he was in Kansas for the centenary celebrations in October 2006. I usually just put them on the table in his room without a word.

The lessons I learned from compiling these books are so many. In *Bhaja Govindam*, for example, Baba discusses the poem by Adi Shankara, which describes the transitory nature of the world. Once, Adi Shankara happened to see an old scholar teaching some students the rules of Sanskrit grammar. Taking pity on the scholar, he went up to him and advised him not to waste his time on grammar at his age but to turn his mind to God in worship and adoration. Out of sympathy for the worn-out old man wasting time with grammar, Shankara spontaneously recited a verse "O ignorant man, sing the glory of Govinda. Your knowledge of grammar will not save you from approaching death. What is the use of memorizing these grammar rules instead of taking refuge in God?" This took the form of a melodious song beginning with the word *Bhaja Govindam,* which means sing the name of God. Baba ended his commentary on this inspired composition by urging us to focus on God, to convert our emotion to devotion and direct our love to God rather than to the transient and changing world.

In his commentary on *Dasha Shloki,* Baba once again interpreted the inspired words of Adi Shankara, this time on the nature of the self. Shankara insists that the barriers of race, religion, caste, nation, obscure the true nature of the self, which is beyond all these. Baba made Shankara's words and message crystal clear by drawing on his vast knowledge of world scripture including the *Yogasutras of Patanjali,* the *Bible,* the *Gita* and the *Upanishads.*

Baba also gave lectures on the *Bhagavatam.* Srimad Bhagavatam is a scripture of supreme love for God and talks of the divine play of the several incarnations of God. There is an interesting back ground as to how this work of Maharshi Vyasa came about. Vyasa is considered the father of Vedic culture who has edited the Vedas and written several books. It is said that even after Maharshi Vyasa had finished writing his prolific works he was still not happy and was one day contemplating sitting on the banks of the river Sarasvati, if he had really achieved what he wanted to do. He felt despondent that something was missing. Just then Sage Narada was passing by and on knowing the cause of Vyasa's sorrow advised him thus, "You have achieved things that no other can do. You are a genius. Your many literary works like the *Mahabharata* deal with *dharma*, *artha* and *kama* and talk about how to attain love, but they lack love and devotion. Write something that will touch the lives of all. A work that people can read or listen to and transform their life. Write the stories of the Lord that invoke divine love. Love liberates."

After completing the Bhagavatam, Vyasa realized that the person who narrated the stories needed to have the special qualities to adequately relay the love contained within their pages. He chose Shuka, his paramahamsa son, for this task.

As Baba regaled us with his own metaphorical interpretations of these divine stories, it was apparent that he was also perfectly suited for the task.

Jnanasankalini

Another great work was the *Tantra* book. *Jnanasankalini Tantra* is presented as a dialogue between Lord Siva and his consort Parvati, who is also his best student. Baba wrote a commentary on the *Jnanasankalini Tantra*, a work that took him many years but emerged as a comprehensive volume that explained the many mysteries, misunderstandings and misinterpretations surrounding the word *tantra*.

Before reading Baba's explanation, I also had many misconceptions about *tantra* and *tantriks*. I imagined them as a strange cult who indulged in drunken orgies in the name of the Goddess. Having understood the practice in the right way thanks to Baba's commentary, I realized that *tantra,* while it may be misinterpreted and misused by some practitioners, was in its purest form just another method of spiritual *sadhana.*

Devi Mahatmya

When we were in Cleveland, Baba talked about the *chandi* also known as *Devi Mahatmya*, a treatise of seven hundred mantras on the glory of the Divine Mother. Until then, although we were familiar with the fact that people recite the *chandi* during the navaratri, and also perform *havan* using the seven hundred mantras, we had never attempted it.

We were thrilled that Baba was showing us yet another way to worship the Goddess, and when Baba was present we asked him if we could perform the fire ceremony under his direction. He agreed and we performed a *chandi havan* for the first time using our fireplace.

I chanted the 700 verses along with Baba and managed to do it well. When I told him that it was my first time, he was surprised. It was also Baba who told us that the nine-day worship of the Divine Mother is celebrated both in spring and autumn.

Baba explained that the vanquishing of the demon Mahishasura and all the other demons supposedly took place during the spring navaratri. The navaratri in the autumn is the celebration of the worship of the Divine Mother by Lord Rama before he set off to war with Ravana. Rama invoked the Divine Mother with worship and was blessed to conquer Ravana.

Once we heard this from Baba, we started performing the *havan* during the navaratri following his direction. We started celebrating the navaratri in the spring also. We were blessed to have many fire ceremonies in our house both in Cleveland and in Kansas during navaratri, which coincided with Baba's visits.

In the beginning, the *chandi* looked to us like a story of battle, with the Goddess fighting with demon after demon to protect the gods against their atrocities. But as we kept reading with Baba's guidance, we began to understand the deeper meaning of the *chandi*.

When Baba said he would write a commentary on the *chandi* in English, we were overjoyed. Baba suggested that we start by typing the verses in *devanagari* script with English transliteration, and to add the translation that Baba had written under the verse. Harinath was so excited, and for a person who is not familiar with Hindi or Sanskrit, he was somehow inspired to figure out all the 700 verses and the transliteration. I went through the inserting of Baba's translation under each transcribed verse. It took quite a few years for Baba to complete this major undertaking but when it finally happened it was a great accomplishment.

In his three-volume commentary on the *chandi*, which was titled *Only Her Grace*, Baba explains how the raging battles actually demonstrate the love of the Mother, who destroys attachments and grants discrimination. He describes the nurturing power of the Mother's threefold aspect, marveling over how She simultaneously awakens the sleeping child, disciplines the restless one, and uplifts the one seeking liberation. It was truly by the Mother's grace and his meditative experiences that Baba was able to achieve this tremendous task.

Baba's various lectures covered a wide variety of topics. He spoke on Hindu scriptures, the Puranas, the Gita, the Upanishads, the Bhakti Sutras, the Yoga Sutras of Patanjali, on treatises like the Yoga Vasishtha and the Chandi, and on the lives of saints and sages. With his profound knowledge of the scriptures of both the East and the West, he also spoke of the Beatitudes (the Sermon on the Mount) and The Path of St Francis. His book, *The Torah, the Bible, and Kriya Yoga,* is an amazing combination of the teachings of many faiths that proves their inherent unity.

The Beginning of Sthita Prajna

In the year 1999, when we were in Hudson, Ohio, Baba was with us for the Kriya Program in Cleveland. During conversation, it came up one day that it would be nice to have a newsletter that would cover the Cleveland Center news and also have an inspiring article to keep people in touch with the teachings of the gurus. That thought resulted in a two-page newsletter being created on our home computer and we thought of calling it Kriyavani but then changed the name to Prajnanavani.

My husband Harinath, my daughter Jyothi, and I worked to put it together. We were the compilers, editors, proofreaders and printers. As with any good work, we faced some criticism and jealousies. Undaunted by criticism and inspired by Baba's talks and his encouragement, we continued to bring out Prajnanavani as an independent newsletter and mailed it to friends free of cost. From time to time, a nice letter from the readers who sincerely appreciated the articles and wrote about how they were benefited, was reward enough and kept us going.

At one of the Gita lectures at the temple, Baba discussed the qualities of sthita prajna, which means one who is established in wisdom. In the Bhagavad Gita, the Lord describes the state that is called sthita prajna. Prajna means wisdom, not just knowledge. There is a difference between the two. Knowledge we all have, but not wisdom. We know what is good and what is bad. This is knowledge. But if we do not apply the knowledge in our daily life, we are only theoretically intelligent.

Baba often explained that knowledge is *jnana*, applied knowledge is *vijnana* and the happiness we get by applying knowledge is wisdom or *prajnana*. Established in *prajnana,* you will never forget the truth at any moment that you are the soul, God is all pervading, God is in all and you will remain continuously in the truth. In summary, a sthita prajna is one who has thorough control over the senses. He is one who is always aware of inner spirit, does everything in the awareness of the soul, and does everything as an offering to God. He works with love, without anxiety or emotion, every moment he works with a sense of sacrifice. After we heard Baba's explanation, we decided we would change the name of the journal to Sthita Prajna.

During a visit to Miami in the year 2000, Baba informed us that disciples in India were feeling the need for a magazine for Prajnana Mission. That led to making Sthita Prajna a quarterly magazine to be distributed both in India and the United States. Since then, the magazine is compiled here in the States and then printed in India. With the cooperation and support of some hardworking disciples and the Graphic Art Offset Press in Cuttack, we were able to coordinate our efforts and in January 2001, Sthita Prajna was printed in India for the first time. With the support of our readers, Sthita Prajna has grown steadily over the years and has taken its present shape as an international magazine with circulation in India, the United States, Europe, Australia and South America.

Gurudev had been reading this magazine with great interest since the very beginning and on March 6, 2001, we were pleasantly surprised to receive a letter of appreciation from him.

INSTITUTE

24757 SW 167ᵗʰ Avenue. Homestead, FL 33031-1364, U.S.A.
TEL. 305-247-1960
FAX. 305-248-1931

THE KRIYA YOGA OF BABAJI, LAHIRI MAHASAYA, SWAMI SHRIYUKTESHWAR, PARAMAHAMSA YOGANANDA & PARAMAHAMSA HARIHARANANDA

March 6, 2001,

My affectionate and Divine Harinath,

I am extremely happy to receive the small book Sthita Prajna. Undoubtedly it is heart touching and it will give reality to mankind.

You all take my deepest affection and enjoy the blessings of God and Gurus.

humble

Swami H. Giri

Hariharananda

5

WITH BABA IN INDIA

I wanted to visit the India ashrams while Baba was in India. I made the trip to India in 1999 when Baba was there. I arrived at the Bhubaneswar airport and was greeted by Mr. Bidyasagar Shah, a long time disciple of Gurudev, who received me and drove me from the airport to the Jagatpur ashram on the outskirts of Cuttack. The road from Bhubaneswar to Cuttack in those days was not a highway and it took us almost two hours to reach the ashram. When we finally reached the gates, I looked up at the big white building and was thrilled to see the sign "Prajnana Mission" in bold blue letters welcoming me. It was a dream come true.

Founding of Prajnana Mission

Baba had returned to India after three years in the West, with the idea of beginning an organization. Gurudev had given his blessings for the founding of Prajnana Mission. The Mission was founded with Swami Brahmananda Giri as the vice president and Swami Shuddhananda Giri as the secretary. A humble monk of profound wisdom, Brahmanandaji was in charge of the Cuttack ashram at the time and toured many Kriya centers in India spreading the message of Kriya Yoga.

First Visit to Cuttack Ashram

As the secretary of Prajnana Mission, Shuddhanandaji was organizing the many activities of the Mission at the Cuttack and Balighai ashrams. He also managed Yuktashram, a beautiful hermitage in Bhisindipur, Bengal.

These two swamis along with Baba as the president were the main pillars of Prajnana Mission. Then there was Swami Arupananda Giri who was initiated in 1996 into monkhood by Gurudev. His simplicity and love accompanied with hard work and service was an inspiration to others.

My Time at the Cuttack Ashram

I had been waiting to see the Cuttack ashram for a long time. The car entered the gates and stopped in front of the porch that leads to the library on one side and the kitchen on the other. There was a beautiful flower garden in front of the building. As we walked towards the library, Baba came out of the library to greet us. My long anticipation of seeing him again and touching his feet was realized at that moment.

We went into the library and joined the group of nearly a dozen people who were there. The large library has a vast collection of scriptures, religious treatises and volumes of books. Baba was using the library as his bedroom. Pointing to a mat in the corner he said, "That is my bed and this is where I sleep." Baba looked thinner and a little fatigued, but his spiritual energy was very apparent in his sparkling eyes and the shine on his forehead. It was so good to see him in his natural surroundings, and I was content to just be there in his presence.

When I came out of the library, I met some other visiting disciples. There was Roland Baba from Germany and another disciple from Poland. Meditation that evening was guided personally by Baba in the large meditation hall on the second floor. The altar has a life-size portrait of Gurudev and pictures of the lineage of gurus. Meditation was followed by a simple nourishing dinner served by the young brahmacharis of the ashram. Baba would eat only after all the guests were fed. There were about 40 people who attended meditation and then stayed for dinner. I went to bed happy to be in the ashram and happy to be part of the mission.

While at the ashram I would get up every morning at 5 a.m. Since the ashram faced east, I enjoyed an unobstructed view of the glorious sunrise around 6:30 a.m. For the morning meditation, Baba walked in with his hair still wet and tied up in a knot, and it struck me how small his physical stature was, compared to his gigantic spiritual stature.

He started the meditation with a beautiful morning prayer composed by Adi Shankara:

Pratah smarami hridi.........

In the pre-dawn hours I meditate on that self in my heart which takes me to the 4th dimension of paramahamsa state, the state of Supreme brahman, beyond the 3 states of wakeful, dream and deep sleep, and beyond elemental existence.

It was a blissful experience to be there that morning listening to the magical voice which makes the meaning of every word he utters come to life. It is that voice which lends new life to the verses, even if one has heard them a hundred times before. Then he guided the meditation, which was a song in itself, as he spoke in both Odia and English, alternating the languages with ease.

I sat with Swami Brahmananda for some time. He narrated how he met Baba first at the Puri ashram and then at Bhubaneswar and how they spent a lot of time together as disciples of Gurudev Hariharanandaji. He described how they always wanted to have an ashram in Cuttack and after searching for a place close to the river, had finally found the present site, which had only a small building on it when Baba first purchased it.

The building has since been extended. It is now a very impressive two-storied white building with a touch of lilac, and is very pretty. The main wing of the ground floor has an enclosed porch, the kitchen, the dining hall and the library and two other small rooms. The side wing has the monks' bedrooms. A very artistically designed outside staircase leads to the second floor, which houses the meditation room and several guest rooms.

After lunch Baba was back in the library, meeting people who came to see him. Swami Suddhananda, the then secretary of Prajnana Mission, arrived with a group of disciples from Poland whom he had received in Kolkata. I was walking in the garden, when I encountered the elderly couple who came to meet Baba that morning. The gentleman was so full of emotion after talking to Baba, he had tears streaming down his face and with a choked voice told me how every single word Baba utters is so inspiring. Nothing new. I have yet to see a person to whom Baba might have said only one word at only one time, who does not feel that way.

There was a talk by Baba in the evening, which was followed by meditation. The devotion of the European disciples was amazing. They had traveled such long distances to come to a country of an entirely different language and culture, only to be with the guru and meditate. In spite of the language problem (they could not speak or understand English) they attended the classes with great discipline. Fortunately, there was one person who could translate English into Polish.

The brahmacharis at the ashram were very loving and friendly. The place was charged with Baba's love for all and with their tremendous love for him. I spent nearly two weeks in this divine atmosphere and realized the truth in the saying that one must be with the guru continuously to fully understand what he is. I thank God for the opportunity.

During that time I sat in the library most of the time as Baba worked. I remember him sitting on a mat in front of the file cabinet taking out old files and dusting each one and sorting them out. There was no one to assist him and there were people coming to see him throughout the day. He managed to continue working while still being pleasant to all those who came, showering them with his love and enquiring about their families.

Watching him at work, I asked, "Is this a one man organization, Baba?" and he smiled. I offered to help, but he said I would not know the files. It was a rare opportunity to see the beginnings of an organization and to be a part of it.

After the meditation that evening, I spent some time with Baba's niece, Annada, a very loving girl who told me about her family, and how they moved from their village to their present residence so she and her brother could go to better schools. She promised to come the next day and take me for a walk up to the river, a branch of Mahanadi which was close by.

I was the only one from the United States staying at the ashram at the time, along with Swami Shuddhananda and Brahmananda, and a few European disciples. Baba's niece, Annada, kept me company and we would walk to the nearby river in the evenings.

One day, with Baba's permission, she took me to lunch at their apartment close by, making her mother cook many special dishes. This girl was getting very attached to me. She has a strong resemblance to Baba and some of the gestures she makes are very similar. Her father Gopinath Kar, was adopted by a close relative when he was still a baby, hence the difference in the last names. He supervised the running of the ashram as a voluntary service, and both he and his wife Kalpana were very devoted disciples of Baba. They were very loving hosts and I could not help thinking how blessed these people were to belong to the same family as Baba. It was also nice to see how the family treated Baba – they loved him dearly and were more like disciples, willing to do anything for him. Annada also had a brother Swaroop whom I met.

Baba guided the morning meditation and then left early with Suddhanandaji on some business, coming back at 10 a.m. We then sat in the library and organized the paperwork for the press. I think it was the book *Prapanna Gita* we were working on. The list of photographs needed to be updated and the pictures for the book covers finalized. Many people came to see him throughout the morning. He would talk to them as he worked.

I was lucky to have Baba's *darshan* very early in the morning, sometimes before the meditation time. Whenever I saw him standing on the balcony, I joined him in watching the sunrise, and we talked for a while. It was a blissful experience seeing the rising sun and the guru both at the same time.

Saraswati Puja

Saraswati Puja is celebrated on a very large scale in Odisha, in all the schools as well as in the homes. As it is considered a very auspicious day, many initiations were scheduled at the ashram that morning.

Initiations were conducted by Baba and Brahmanandaji. Annada took initiation that day. It was nice to see this young girl dressed in new clothes getting initiated by her saintly uncle. After the initiations, the fire ceremony was a full-scale *havan* by Baba.

The whole process of *havan* was explained as it was performed. The significance of water, leaves, flowers, coconut, ghee and cloth were all explained. The firewood symbolizing the gross body is burned with the help of ghee or clarified butter. Ghee symbolizes purity or divine love. Baba emphasized that just bringing the wood and ghee together does not cause the fire. The friction or interaction of two pieces of wood causes the fire. This is the fire of knowledge produced by the interaction of the teacher and the student. This is the external or the symbolic fire ceremony. Baba reminded us that the real fire ceremony is the ongoing one in which the *prana* or breath is offered as an oblation into the fire in the cranium, which results in *samadhi* or bliss.

As soon as the *havan* was completed and *prasad* distributed, we rushed to another location where Baba was invited to give a discourse. This was the house of a devotee of Sathya Sai Baba, where a special puja was performed in connection with Saraswati puja, followed by *bhajan* and then Baba was to speak. As always it was a beautiful talk. The lecture was in Odia, but amazingly understandable. Either I must have become familiar with the Odia language for the past four days, since I had never heard this language before this trip, or language was not a barrier when you are really tuned in. I could get most of the talk written down in English as it was being delivered in Odia. As usual, Baba as the chief guest was asked to perform the *arati* for Sathya Sai, which he graciously did. This personally had a great significance for me.

I had always felt that it was Sathya Sai who directed me to the present guru and to witness my guru offering *arati* to Sai Baba somehow confirmed that thought.

✳ ✳ ✳ ✳ ✳ ✳ ✳ ✳ ✳ ✳ ✳ ✳ ✳ ✳ ✳ ✳ ✳ ✳ ✳

Meeting Sathya Sai

I was in high school when I first heard of Sri Sathya Sai Baba. This was about the time when his miracle manifestations were coming into public awareness. In one of our teachers' houses, *vibhuti* (sacred ash) was appearing on his photograph and also on the fruits that were offered as *prasad*. This was the talk of the school. I remember going to the teacher's house along with my mother and listening to their account. I remember Mother being surprised at someone saying how Sai Baba claims he is God. She was shocked at how a man could claim to be God and after much discussion, our parents decided to go and visit him in Puttaparthi. I also remember Mother saying, "If I can see this person who says he is God with my own eyes, I can make my final judgment." So they left for Puttaparthi, and I remember eagerly waiting for their return. When they came back, having seen some of the miracles for themselves and having listened to Sai Baba speak, they were fully convinced of his divinity. I remember her saying with firm conviction, "Yes, he is God. There is no doubt about it."

Once my parents were convinced and had full faith, the picture of Sai Baba was added to the altar and worshipped on Thursdays. Both my mother and father had great faith in Sathya

Sai Baba and during the years that followed, we all visited Puttaparthi, had interviews with Sai Baba, and the whole family was devoted and considered Sathya Sai both a guru and God.

Later on, Father also converted an extra storeroom in the house into a temple for Sai, which had both the photos of Sathya Sai Baba and Shirdi Sai Baba in it. Shirdi Baba is believed to be the previous incarnation of Sathya Sai Baba. It was customary in Puttaparthi, that any devotee in difficulty or crisis or even before doing something important or auspicious thing in life would write a letter to Sai Baba and sit in the *darshan* lines holding the letter. Sai Baba walked the lengthy lines, stopping here and there, collecting the letters of the devotees. The devotees had great joy when their letter was taken, and believed that their problem would be solved by the grace of God. Even when a letter was not taken, they had faith that Sai Baba knew what they had come for and they mailed him the letter before they left Puttaparthi. When unable to go to Puttaparthi in person, people would write a letter anyway, and either mail it or keep it near the picture of Sai Baba in their homes with the same faith. Father followed this practice throughout his life, all the way to the end. He always wrote a letter and kept it near Sai Baba's picture before taking up any new project, or whenever faced with resolving a problem. In the course of time, all the children also followed the same thing.

Concept of an Avatar

Sathya Sai Baba was our first introduction to the concept of an *avatar*, an incarnation of God in human form, at least in real life. Though we believed that Lord Rama and Krishna were incarnations of God, it was different when they were distant figures from a past age. When an incarnation is on earth as an apparently contemporary human in all respects, it is hard to believe that he or she is God. It was the same with most people during the time of Lord Rama, Krishna and Jesus. Not everyone could fully believe in them. Even if we intellectually understand that we are all God in human form, it is hard to accept someone who has fully realized his divinity. It could be that it is the *maya* of the Lord, as I later learned, which covers our intelligence. The Lord reveals himself only to those who have faith. It is believed that God himself comes down in the form of the guru out of his love for humanity, to guide us along the path of spirituality. Later, when my understanding matured as I grew up, it did not seem impossible that the compassionate Lord could actually come down to earth to guide his children.

I remember my first visit to Puttparthi. It was in the late 1950s. We travelled by train, bus, and finally bullock cart to reach Puttaparthi. There were a handful of devotees sitting on the sand in front of the building in the *darshan* line and we all excitedly joined the line. Sai Baba walked out and passed by the lines, looking intensely at the people assembled there. When his eyes fell on me and he looked into my eyes, I did not know what happened. I started crying and the tears kept flowing nonstop. It was a feeling of being thoroughly cleansed. I cried silently for quite some time and I remember him looking at me once again.

The next morning we were in line again and we were called for an interview with Sai Baba. We went in as a group - my parents, my sister Radha, and I. He talked to each one of us. By then I had read some of his lectures, and also had some understanding of the Gita. I remembered reading that the most important way to reach God is through *chitta shuddhi,* purity of mind, because God manifested only in pure minds and hearts. When he looked at me, I said, "Baba, I want *chitta shuddhi.*" He smiled and said, *"manchi uddesam bangaru, tappaka avutundi"*- (it is a good wish, my dear, it will definitely come true).

We went to Puttaparthi quite a few times after that and over the years, the Sai organization grew so big that the entire world started coming to Sai. My sister Radha was fortunate in becoming a committed disciple in the capacity of a medical doctor. She had some special visions even before her wedding, and knew her mission was with Sai. In the course of time, she was married to Ravi, my husband's younger brother, who was also a doctor and together they served at the hospital in Puttaparthi and became great devotees of Sai. Even after her wedding, we visited Puttaparthi together a few times. We had some nice experiences of his all-knowing nature. Many questions were answered during visits to Puttaparthi, whether we had an interview or not.

Later, I learned that my husband's family had their own experiences of coming into contact with Sai Baba. Their first contact was a visit to Shirdi, to visit Sai Baba there. There is an interesting connection here as Puttaparthi Sai Baba claimed that Shirdi Baba is his previous incarnation and Prema Sai would be his future incarnation.

When my husband was eight or nine years old, his younger brother Ravi became very sick with pneumonia and was hallucinating and talking away in his high fever. He said he saw Shirdi Sai Baba. At that time his parents had never heard of Shirdi Baba and had no idea where Shirdi was. But they prayed and pledged to visit Shirdi after Ravi recovered. He soon got better and they made their first trip to Shirdi about sixty years ago. In those days, transportation and local arrangements were minimal. They went by train for some distance, then by bus, and finally by bullock cart to reach Shirdi. They had a good *darshan* and went back several times after that. From that first trip to many more trips later, they always had front row *darshan* and a comfortable stay at Shirdi by the grace of Shirdi Baba.

Later still, when the family was in Penukonda in Anantapur District and my husband was about fourteen years old, they heard of Sathya Sai Baba and went to Puttaparthi for his *darshan* for the first time. There were no large crowds in Puttaparthi during that time. They reached late in the evening, were accommodated in a nice room, and had the privilege of having dinner served by the divine mother of Sai Baba, Eshwaramma herself. The next morning, they had *darshan* of Sai Baba in a private room. He blessed them all. He materialized *vibhuti* and a locket and gave these to my husband's father.

We all come with different missions in life. In later years, as I kept meeting different spiritual masters, I felt they were all connected and fitted beautifully into the divine cosmic drama and the grand scheme of things. Different people come to serve different masters in their limited capacities, but it seems there is a director and prompter behind the scenes. I have and still do pray to Sai Baba as a guru and guide and also firmly believe that it is he who has directed me to wherever I am meant to be in life.

✳ ✳ ✳ ✳ ✳ ✳ ✳ ✳ ✳ ✳ ✳ ✳ ✳ ✳ ✳ ✳ ✳ ✳ ✳ ✳

We returned to the Cuttack ashram after the program. Baba conducted a two-hour class for the new initiates that afternoon. He had no rest since early that morning, was fasting, conducted a three hour ceremony in the morning, gave a discourse in the afternoon, and now he was teaching a class. He also guided the meditation in the evening. Where he gets such energy, I cannot imagine. He gives and gives. All you can do is to pray to God to take care of him. We finally had dinner at 9:45 p.m. and went to bed.

Baba as My Guide

Busy as he was, Baba took time to take me with him as much as possible to show me places in Cuttack and Puri. I went to the press in Cuttack with Baba and Shuddhanandaji. From there we went to Bhubaneswar, to the bank, and on the way back, stopped at a disciple's house. We came back to the ashram and had lunch. I was getting very used to the Odia food.

Another day I was able to accompany Baba on a trip to Bhubaneswar and Puri. We went along with another elderly gentleman who had come from Puri to see Baba at the Cuttack ashram. As we headed towards Puri, we crossed over the bridge of Mahanadi into Cuttack. We drove through different areas of Cuttack and as it was my first visit, Baba was pointing out different buildings like the stadium and the high court and he said, "I am your guide today." I replied, "You are my guide always, Baba." He smiled and said, "I mean a travel guide."

Baba gave me a good tour of Cuttack. The first stop was at a Chandi temple. The goddess is known as Cuttack Chandi, a small idol, very beautiful and considered a very powerful deity. It was a great feeling to visit God under the guidance of the Guru. There were smaller temples of Hanuman and Ganesh within the main temple. Then we were on the main road known as the Cantonment Road, which housed many administrative buildings and office buildings. We passed by a big old fort, which was now in a dilapidated condition and was being renovated, and then drove by a huge air-conditioned stadium.

Visit to Jagannath Temple

We finally reached Puri and after dropping the gentleman at his home, we proceeded to the famed Jagannath temple. As we neared the temple, Baba shared with me some of his love for Jagannath and some of the interesting personal experiences he had at the temple.

There are different stories about Lord Jagannath coming to Puri. History has it that he was originally a tribal deity, adored by the Shabara tribe as a symbol of Narayana. Another legend claims him to be Nilamadhava, an image of Narayana made of iridescent blue stone and worshipped by the aboriginals. He was brought to Nilagiri or Nilachala meaning blue mountain and installed there as Shri Jagannath in company with Balabhadra and Subhadra.

The present images are made of wood. The daitapatis, who are mostly responsible for performing rituals at the temple, are claimed to be descendants of the original hill tribes of Odisha. So the cultural history of the temple is based on a fusion of Hindu and tribal cultures. Lord Jagannath is worshipped as Vishnu or Narayana or Krishna, with his brother Lord Balabhadra as Shesha and sister Subhadra. Bhairava (Lord Siva) and Bhairavi (the consort of Siva) are also installed in the campus of the temple.

Baba has great love for Lord Jagannath and at one time during conversation, Baba had said, "Lord Jagannath is the reason for my being born in Odisha." At another time he also said, "Jagannath temple is my field of meditation."

The culture of Odisha is heavily intertwined with Lord Jagannath. He is part of every household and is lovingly referred to as Kalia. Baba told us many interesting family stories of the Lord —of his divine consort Lakshmi getting angry and breaking the wheel of the chariot on the *rathayatra* day and how she does not let him get back into the main temple after the *rathayatra* because she was not asked to accompany him. Many of these stories are re-enacted during the chariot festival and are very interesting to watch.

As we made our way through the streets, Lord Jagannath's temple could be seen in the distance. It is a huge towering temple complex. Baba led us through the many smaller temples that surrounded the main temple. There are quite a few Shakti temples including that of Goddess Vimala. There are also the temples of Rama, Hanuman, Ganesha and the Navagrahas. Then we visited the temple of the Goddess Lakshmi, the consort of Lord Jagannath. In the Jagannath temple, the temple of Lakshmi is separate from the main temple. Although I had some ideas as to what the deities looked like, I had no idea how huge they were. It was a nice *darshan* and standing there in front of the deities with Baba reminded me of what I read about the *guru Govinda darshan*. It is said that it is of great significance to see the Lord in the company of one's guru, as the guru shows the way to reach the Lord. I bowed to Baba as soon as we came out of the main temple.

Karar Ashram

Immediately after our visit to the temple, we left for the Karar ashram of Shriyukteshwar. We drove by the seashore and reached the ashram. The ashram has three different buildings. One is the present meditation hall. The second building has the original meditation place used during the time of Shriyukteshwar, which is now closed, and the living quarters in the rear. Baba showed us the room in which Gurudev lived for a long period at first as a *brahmachari* and later as a monk and head of the Karar ashram. Directly above that room is the room in which Baba stayed as

Brahmachari Triloki Baba and served his guru while he was working in Ravenshaw College in Cuttack. Baba showed us the small room in which Mahavatar Babaji gave *darshan* to Hariharanandaji.

The third building was the samadhi mandir of Shriyukteshwar. Inside is a big marble statue of Swami Shriyukteshwar with a Sivalinga in front of it. We sat in the *mandir* for a few minutes. It is a very tranquil place and one can feel the strong spiritual vibration. At the ashram, we met Vimal Baba from Kolkata and another disciple from Vienna. Later, Baba explained to me that his initiation into *sannyas* took place in the house of Vimal Baba.

Balighai Ashram

Vimal Baba accompanied us to the Balighai ashram property, which was our next stop. Gurudev had acquired this beautiful piece of land close to the sea hoping for it to be an International Kriya Yoga Ashram. He enriched the property and it is a really beautiful place with hundreds of coconut and mango groves.

He also planned for a beautiful building with arches which was constructed to the roof level in the 1980's. There were stairs going up to the terrace that would be the future meditation hall. There was a small free-standing cottage with a picture of Gurudev in it which was used for meditation. There were also a couple of rooms near the gate where two brahmacharis lived to take care of the grounds.

In 1996, Gurudev transferred the property to Baba's name after being directed by Shriyukteshwarji in a dream that the place would grow into a beautiful ashram and a place of international reputation in the future through Baba.

We walked the grounds and came back to the small house near the gate. They had green coconuts cut for us and we had the sweetest coconut water I had ever tasted.

From there, after dropping Vimal Baba off at his hotel, we proceeded to the ashram of the famous Nanga Baba. It is located on the top of a small hill and is known as Advaita Brahmashram. There is a large room with four big photographs of the monk in four different postures and in the back is another room where he lived, with a big chair which he used during his life time. The main *mandir* has a statue of the monk. The whole place had a very tranquil atmosphere and it felt very good to sit there for some time to meditate, especially in the presence of Baba. Later, Baba mentioned how as a young boy he was strangely attracted to the picture of this monk in a store and purchased it without even knowing who he was.

Mahaprasad

We returned to the Jagannath temple that evening. When we came out of the main temple we found out that there was still an hour's wait for the *mahaprasad*. We spent some time looking around a few bookstores and went back to the temple and managed to get a place to sit on one of the temple verandahs. The starlit sky was of a clear blue color. Looking up, you could see the main *sikhara*, the highest point of the temple, with the chakra and the flag. The moon was directly above on the top of the *sikhara*. There was a group of brahmacharis reciting the Purusha Sukta, a Vedic hymn, right behind us. It was a blessed moment.

Finally, *mahaprasad* was available. Ananda Bazar is a sight to see. It is located within the temple courtyard and is the place where the *mahaprasad* is distributed. It is hard to describe the hundreds and thousands of earthenware pots of every shape and size filled with hot steaming food cooked on the temple premises, offered to Jagannath, and then sold to the waiting devotees.

The crowd was so big that people sat anywhere and everywhere they could to eat. With great difficulty we managed to get a spot to sit right behind a food stall. Four of us sat huddled together in a small place hardly big enough for the banana leaves on which we ate. Baba served the hot steaming food with his own hands. The food was super hot and very tasty, especially after the day's fast. Rice and many kinds of vegetables and lentils and sweet dishes were there. It was the best meal one could ever eat. Baba explained that the *mahaprasad* of Jagannath is believed to be very sacred and enhances one's devotion. He told us that Sri Ramakrishna Paramahamsa once mixed a few grains of the Jagannath *prasad* in the food of Swami Vivekananda, who was against idol worship, just to increase his devotion.

After this very satisfying meal, I found myself in that ancient sacred temple sitting near the feet of my guru. My heart was filled with supreme peace and happiness, like I did not need anything else in the world. I sat there and meditated and thought of every member of the family and prayed for their spiritual progress. This was a rare privilege. I thanked God and thought, "I must have done something right to deserve this," and prayed and hoped to be on the right track under the guidance of this loving guru.

I was so thankful for that day and to Baba for taking the time out from a very busy schedule to spend the whole day showing me all these sacred places. On the way back, he said, "My schedule is so tight, I wanted to show you as much as possible today. If time permits we can come back to the temple again, but it does not seem possible this month." I did not worry about it. After this day, I thought, I will not ask him for anything. Anything extra will only be a bonus. With great love, he asked each of us if anyone was tired. The young man who was driving the car replied in Odia, "With you seated in the car, how can I be tired?" These were my thoughts exactly.

Baba started singing songs on the way back. We reached the ashram around 10.30 p.m. It was a very memorable day. Since then I went to Jagannath Temple quite a few times with Baba. He looked different, completely transformed, whenever he entered the temple, like he was in communion with God. The humility with which he visited each deity and bowed down was amazing to see. Some of the times we would have enough time to go to Ananda Bazar and eat the *mahaprasad,* and at other times we could only manage the *darshan.*

As the years passed, Baba's time was becoming very limited, but he never missed seeing Jagannath on every visit, several times. Sometimes he would go to the temple very late at night and sometimes very early in the morning. On every visit, impossible as it seemed, my wish to go to the temple with Baba was granted. Lord Jagannath listened to my prayer and I could go at least once during every visit. I even had the opportunity to be present in Puri during the Chariot Festival, when millions of people attend the festival with great devotion and religious fervor. Baba was in the forefront along wth Swami Shuddhananda and helped drag the chariot forward for a few paces.

Miraculous Moments

Baba had his own unique experiences with the Lord, which he very rarely shared. It was his habit whenever he came back to India to first visit Jagannath temple and then take his meals. Once, he related a magical story of his experience while visiting Jagannath temple.

I went back from Europe, to India, it was during the chariot festival. The Lord Jagannath was in the other temple. I landed in Bhubaneswar, and came to Cuttack to see two people who were critically ill and hospitalized. One was just on death's door and after my visit he left his body. At that time there was a telephone call from Puri that the temple would be closing soon. Whenever I go to Puri, I go to Jagannath temple, I offer my prayers and only then I take food. Sometimes I first go to Balighai, visit Gurudev, and then to Jagannath temple or first to Jagannath temple and then Gurudev, depending upon the time. This time they said the temple will be closed at eight o'clock and no one would be allowed inside, as they would start coloring the deities.

Do you know what happened? We went into the temple campus. The temple was closed. As it was during the Rathayatra festival when millions of people visit Puri, there was tight security, with hundreds of police. So I bowed down from the outside of the main temple inside the temple campus. Then I said to Swami Brahmananda who was with me, "Ok. May be today Lord Jagannath doesn't want us to take food."

There is a traditional belief that if somebody is offering the food from the temple, you do not refuse it. The food of Jagannath temple is respected almost more than the deity. Brahmanandaji and I were standing in a corner. It was dark. Suddenly a man appeared whom I had not seen before. He was also of a dark complexion. He said, "Hey Babaji", in a very playful way, not with respect, not with disrespect, in just a friendly manner. "Hey Babaji, you want to go inside?" he repeated.

I said, "Yes, but the temple is closed, isn't it?" He said, "It is closed for everybody, not for you. Wait, wait, wait. Wait here, you will have *darshan*."

So I stood in the corner with Brahmanandaji. He went somewhere and brought nice warm food and put it in my hands. It was very delicious spicy rice and he asked me to eat. Then he gave some to Brahmanandaji also. Now I was in conflict, as I wanted to see Jagannath and then take food. If I ate now, would I be able to see Jagannath or not? This man kept assuring me that I will get the *darshan* but it seemed next to impossible. But to disrespect this prasad, which we call *mahaprasad,* the great sanctified food, is also not good. "Eat. What are you thinking? Eat!" said our friend again. Then I ate.

He went another three or four times like this, each time bringing handfuls of food and giving it to us. It was a good meal. Then he went and brought some water to wash our hands. He said, "You stand here. Three painters will go inside to paint the deities. And when three painters go, you two will go along with them." He said this with a lot of confidence and he disappeared somewhere.

We were standing there a little distance from the closed temple door. At the moment when the three painters arrived, a priest whom I had never seen before was holding our hands and said, "You babas, you are to go." Before we knew what was happening, we were inside the temple. The two priests, the two monks and the three painters. There was no one else. Usually nobody is allowed during that time when the painters are painting. We were standing inside the temple and I was thinking, "O God, it is all you. If you want to do something, You can do it. You can make the impossible possible. Sometimes when we plan and think it is all very easy, if you don't want, it will not happen. You wanted to play with me because of my ego. I was determined that first I will see Lord Jagannath, then I will take food, and if there will be no *darshan*, I will not take food today. You wanted to change my view, and said first you eat and then you will see me.

After hearing this magical story, whenever I was at Balighai ashram I would request that all of us go to the temple with Baba to have *mahaprasad* there, and most of the time my wish would materialize.

Republic Day

January 26th was Republic Day in India. It was a holiday. Many visitors came to the ashram from early in the morning. One of them was Aravinda, with his wife Deepika and their three children, together with another young couple Debi Baba and his wife, who were their close friends. Both Aravinda and his wife were Baba's classmates in his postgraduate economics class. They were seeing him after many years and for the first time as a monk.

They had many questions about his life, what he taught, and what he did in America and Europe.

After talking to him for some time, both the ladies became very interested in getting initiated into Kriya Yoga. The men hesitated a bit and had more questions, but that did not last very long. They stayed for most of the day and it was very interesting to see with how much love Baba treated them and played with the children. There were many others besides these two families. We all sat in the library and Baba patiently answered everyone's questions. Everyone stayed for lunch and after lunch we sat in the library again. Baba peeled oranges and individually fed each person. It was one of those moments when he was overflowing with love and compassion.

I was reminded of another time after the regional retreat in August in Ohio. A three-day spiritual retreat had just ended and most of the people had already left. A close disciple who had recently returned from India had brought Baba *prasad* from Jagannath temple in Puri. When I walked into his room for something, he offered me the *prasad*. I stretched out my palm as usual, but to my surprise he fed me the *prasad*. With great joy and surprise, I bowed at his feet. Later, my husband and daughter related the same experience. We were all happy for this special blessing that he had given us.

After the first batch of people left on Republic Day, people from the surrounding areas and people from the village took over. The love of these people was something else to watch. They had no inhibitions. Whatever he might be to the outside world, he was their own child. They made him lie down and each of them started massaging his feet, hands, head and shoulders, all at the same time. There was the little frame of Baba, surrounded on all sides, each of his limbs in the hands of a loving devoted mother. He talked to each of them, inquiring about their families and responding to their jokes. After half an hour of giving them their share of pleasure, he was up again for the afternoon discourse session. No nap, no rest, just continuous talking.

During the afternoon discourse, Baba talked about hypocrisy and asked everyone to examine themselves to see if they were really what they seemed to be. He said, "When a fruit ripens, it changes both inside and outside. Only outward change does not help. Just donning the garb of a *sannyasi* does not make one spiritual. External show is not important. One's mind should change for the better. Question yourself constantly. Are you the body, the mind or the soul? Meditation is not for the body and it is not needed for the soul. Meditation is for the mind. Mind is between the body and the soul and unless the mind is controlled, you cannot reach the soul." He added, "Watch the mind to see what type of thoughts are going through it and try to keep it clean. Be God conscious and try to perceive God in everyone." He concluded the talk with a beautiful song.

After the talk, Baba continued guiding the meditation. When he guides meditation, no matter how tired he is, he conducts a fully guided meditation with every little detail, speaking both in Odia and English. Another disciple translated it to Polish for the Poland disciples.

There was no electricity that evening, and the meditation was done by candlelight. It was a beautiful night outside with plenty of moonlight. Baba sat outside in the yard after meditation again, surrounded by a few disciples. Finally the lights came on, and too exhausted to eat, he went to bed without dinner.

Meeting Baba's Parents at Pattamundai

Visit to Pattamundai

Finally, after a couple of weeks at the ashram, it was time to visit Pattamundai. I was really looking forward to seeing the birthplace of Baba. I wondered what determined the birthplace of saints and yogis and I was also excited to see the parents who had given birth to such a special soul. We left in two cars along with Baba, Shuddhanandaji, Brahmanandaji, Gopi Baba, Roland Baba from Europe and Annada. On the way, we stopped at Baldev Mandir of Kendrapara.

Kendrapara is a small town on the bank of river Gobari, famous for the Baldev Temple that attracts a large number of devotees throughout the year. The annual car festival of Lord Jagannath, Balabhadra and Subhadra is also observed here with great pomp and splendor. Baldev Mandir has the same three deities as in Jagannath Mandir but the idol of Lord Balabhadra is bigger than that of Lord Jagannath, as he is the presiding deity here.

Baba's family had some connection with the priests of the temple, so we were treated with special attention. The *darshan* was beautiful. Any time I would go to a temple with Baba, I felt it was a special experience and after bowing to the deities, bowed to him in the temple. After *darshan,* we rested in a small cottage close by, and a couple of priests brought the *prasad* to the cottage and served us. It was a delicious lunch and for the first time I tasted *rasavali*, a special sweet that is made in the temple.

From ancient times, cloves or *lavang* have been used as a breath freshener and digestive aid in India. Baba had the habit of eating a clove after every meal. It became my special duty to keep a few cloves on hand wherever we traveled, and I would provide them to Baba as well as the other monks. As a result, Swami

Brahmananda fondly dubbed me Lavang Ma. This time, I had forgotten to take the *lavang* with me. I went out to see if I could buy some, and luckily found a small shop where I could procure a few.

Later, Annada and I sat massaging Baba's feet for a few minutes. Massaging the guru's feet gives a special pleasure that is hard to describe. It becomes an opportunity to serve; an opportunity to express gratitude for all the selfless guidance and wisdom a guru imparts, and affords physical closeness to the divinity within the teacher. It becomes a chance to touch the living embodiment of the countless idols we bow to from a distance in every temple, the invisible God we pray to in every church, and the formless spirit revered in all religions. However much we console ourselves with the idea that the formless God is everywhere, for some of us, serving the Guru as God in human form is a tangible means of feeling God's presence beside us. In those early days, there were more opportunities for such service as the crowds around him were less.

From Kendrapara, we continued to Pattamundai. We made a stop at the M.N High School, the very school that Baba had attended as a young man. Some of his teachers were still there. They were very excited to see their student come back as a world teacher. One of them spoke about how Baba, while always remaining respectful, would sometimes ask challenging questions in class that even they could not answer. We took a tour of the school, and Baba noticed that there was no library. This would become his next project, and very soon a well-stocked library would be established at the school.

Close to the school, there is a small *mandir* dedicated to Lord Jagannath. While we visited the temple, Baba spoke to a few people who were interested in renovating it. He would later help them turn it into a large and active temple. In this way, Baba sought to help the schools, the temples and the villages he visited whenever he saw the need.

Then we finally headed for Pattamundai village. There is the town of Pattamundai, which is more developed and is a business center, and a little removed from it is Pattamundai village. It had narrow roads and rich greenery. There were so many flower and fruit trees that it was like passing through a forest preserve. After a certain distance, Baba stopped the car, got down, and started walking. On the way, he stopped at some houses to greet the people. He was seeing them after a few years. He stopped to wipe the tears of some, and had a loving word for all whom he met.

We stopped at a small Siva temple beside a canal, in front of which was a huge banyan tree. As a schoolboy, Baba would sit under this same banyan tree, studying during the summer holidays. People used to come from long distances to do *abhisheka* and worship Lord Siva and sometimes the priest would not be there. Little Triloki, as he was then known, knew the ways of worship to some extent and seeing the disappointment of the devotees, volunteered to do the *puja*. The priest usually left him a key and changing into an orange *dhoti*, which he kept beside him for just such emergencies, Triloki opened the temple doors and carried buckets of water from the canal to give the Lord the ceremonial bath, uttering the mantras to the best of his ability.

Baba had told us these incidents back in Ohio and it was wonderful to be able to see the tree and the temple from that story. We now entered the very same Siva temple and offered our prayers.

Then we proceeded towards the house. Before the entrance was the *mandir* of the family deity Radha Kanta. A few of the family members had assembled in front of the *mandir*. Baba went in to perform *arati* and bowed to the deities and then walked towards the house, where the ladies assembled to wash his feet. After that we went inside.

The home had a hall set up for meditation, with an altar with Gurudev's picture and the lineage of Masters. I met Baba's sister and his other brothers. It was nice to see the parents who bore such a beautiful son. I bowed to them and sat with Mother Vaidehi, who was at once loving and affectionate. I had brought clothes for his parents and I handed them over to Baba to be presented to them, which they accepted gracefully and wore for my satisfaction. I was really happy.

We were treated with a lot of love and affection and they presented clothes to Baba, to Shuddhanandaji, to Roland Baba, and a saree to me. They insisted on my wearing the saree before I left the home and I did. After dinner, we left for Cuttack. Mother Vaidehi came up to the car and bid goodbye with tears in her eyes. "Do not forget me," she said. "You are all his mothers now." It was a memorable visit. We returned to Cuttack by midnight.

Since then I have gone to Pattamundai on most of my visits to India. Usually in January, Baba would go for a visit. And as the number of disciples grew, we all went with him and the family would treat us to a delicious lunch. This became an annual ritual.

Snana Purnima

In the same year, I went to Cuttack again, along with my husband. We went a couple of days ahead of Baba. This time we traveled by train from Hyderabad. We reached Cuttack station around noon, where Swami Arupananda received us and took us to the ashram. The same afternoon, we left for Balighai with Shuddhanandaji.

That was our first overnight stay at Balighai. The ashram grounds had an unspoiled beauty. There were a couple of rooms at the entrance that were being used by the brahmacharis who were taking care of the premises. We slept in one of those small rooms at the entrance. There was no electricity or generators, and the only source of light was the kerosene lamps. Shuddhanandaji went to sleep on the terrace of the meditation hall. The night was so silent – you could even here the insects and some frogs croaking. In the middle of the night, I woke up to hear a frog right under my bed. Still, it was beautiful and in the morning my husband prophesied, "This might be a place where I would like to retire. It is so quiet."

The next morning, we drove to the sea that was only five miles away and bathed there, at the most beautiful private beach. From there we went to the Jagannath temple with Shuddhanandaji. It was the day of *snana purnima,* when once a year, on the full moon day in the month of *jyeshta* (June), the deities from the Jagannath temple are brought out, and are given a holy bath. The deities were on a high platform and could be seen from everywhere. After a long wait, we finally had the chance to have a close *darshan* of the deities. We could go touch and hug them. It was the experience of a lifetime. I hugged each of those massive idols as far as my hands could reach and thanked Baba for making it possible, though he could not be actually present. From the next day, the temple would be closed. We collected some *tirtha* (holy water) in a bottle for Baba and went back to Balighai ashram. The next day we went back to Cuttack and then to Bhubaneswar to receive Baba at the airport.

Charitable Health Centers

With the blessings of Gurudev, a new epoch in the history of Kriya Yoga was ushered in with the opening of two charitable health centers in Cuttack and Balighai ashrams in July of 1999. The centers were opened under the auspices of the Prajnana Mission, to render service to humanity through offering free medical care to hundreds of people in rural areas with no convenient medical facilities. Gurudev sent his blessings and good wishes. It was a nice celebration and lunch was served on the terrace above the meditation hall. It was amazing how Baba was getting so much work done in India while still travelling tirelessly abroad as well as writing prolifically. The progress achieved at the Balighai ashram was simply superhuman.

World Parliament of Religions

Baba was invited to speak at the World Parliament of Religions held in South Africa in December of 1999. He gave two discourses on the topics of yoga and poverty. A small booklet titled *Reaching the Summit,* with a cover picture of Baba at Kedarnath with snow capped Himlayan peaks in the background, was used as an introduction to Kriya Yoga and the lineage of Masters at the Parliament of Religions. Baba was spreading the Kriya message far and wide.

Inauguration of Hariharananda Gurukulam and IIKYS

I was traveling to India whenever Baba was there. The way Prajnana Mission was expanding, it was a pleasure and an inspiration to be present for every accomplishment. I went again in January 2000. The efforts of Baba resulted in yet another milestone in the history of Kriya Yoga. A new building complex was inaugurated in Balighai, Puri. The new ashram,

Hariharananda Gurukulam, was to be managed by Prajnana Mission. The First International Intensive Kriya Yoga Seminar was planned at the Gurukulam. The construction of the meditation hall and a few rooms below were just completed.

I arrived in Cuttack on January 13th, just a day before the inauguration. Baba greeted me with a smile and asked, "Will you stay at the hotel with the others or at the ashram? I do not know how the arrangements are. I have also not seen it yet." I wasn't sure. We reached Balighai late at night. All the European disciples were sent to the nearby hotels. Some Indian disciples were staying at the ashram. When we arrived, the arrangements were not complete and the water connection was not yet in place. There was no electricity, only generators. Things looked a little bleak considering a retreat was to begin the next day.

Baba suggested that I go to the hotel. I was reluctant. Fortunately, Dr. Satyabhama Ma, a long time disciple, offered to take me to a guesthouse where she was staying. With Baba's permission, I went with her and stayed there. By the time we returned the next day, things were pretty much taken care of and everything was in operable condition. Later, those who were there at night said it was almost a miracle how the water supply went on in the middle of the night. Still, there were no rooms available, as the few rooms were given to yogacharyas and guests, and Baba himself was sleeping in the small old meditation room along with the other monks. The women disciples were sleeping in the main meditation hall and the men on the open terrace above, with a temporary canopy overhead. I told Baba again that I wanted to be in the ashram, and he said I could stay in the meditation hall, but that it might be difficult with the wait for the bathrooms. I was determined to try. Luckily, Ambika, a fellow disciple who is now a monk, was with me helping in every way, and within a day I was able to adjust.

On the 14th of January, the auspicious day of Makara Sankranti, fulfilling the much-cherished wish of Gurudev Paramahamsa Hariharananadaji, the inaugural function started with a *havan* in the morning conducted by Paramahamsa Prajnanananda on the flower-bedecked stage, under the benevolent gaze of the lineage of Kriya Masters whose life-size portraits adorned the walls.

The remote ashram grounds of Balighai reverberated with the song led by Paramahamsa Prajnanananda,

Harirevajagat jagadeko hari.....

"Behold the unity in diversity. To see the presence of God in everything and every being is establishment of Truth. God and His creation are not separate. The one who realizes and rejoices in this, is the one who reaches the goal."

Disciples from all over the world who congregated for the Inauguration of Hariharananada Gurukulam and the International Intensive Kriya Yoga Seminar (IIKYS) organized by Prajnana Mission joined in the chorus.

The serene and beautiful ashram grounds of Balighai were sanctified that day by the presence of saints and sages who were invited to grace the occasion and the many spiritual seekers who came from all corners of the globe to quench their spiritual thirst. Swami Srimad Satchidananda Saraswati of Puri, Swami Virajananada Giri of Sevayatan Sastsang Mission of West Bengal, Swami Kaivalyanandaji, Swami Chidanandaji Maharaj of the Divine Life Society, Rishikesh, the Jagadguru Shankaracharya of

Gobardhan Peeth Puri and Gajapathi Maharaja, the King of Puri, were a few of the many holy personalities who decorated the dais during the ten day festival and gave their invaluable message to the assembled seekers. They all paid their homage to Gurudev Paramahamsa Hariharananada and lauded the efforts of Prajnananandaji as the Bhagiratha of modern times who succeeded in bringing the Kriya Ganga to Balighai, to Purushottam Dham, the holy land of Jagannath. The King of Puri cordially welcomed the delegates of the East and the West and expressed the hope that this retreat would become an annual feature at Balighai.

Working around the clock, humbly receiving his guests and presiding over the ceremonies was Baba, the worthy disciple of the worthy guru, whose labor of love is a testimonial to what strong determination, faith in God and Guru, and true spirituality can achieve. A child with children, a friend, philosopher and guide all in one, a mother and a father and a most loving teacher, he taught and inspired by his presence and his example. Assisted by Swami Brahmananada Giri, Swami Shuddhananda Giri, and Swami Arupananada Giri, he was guiding meditations, answering questions, giving discourses, leading songs and serving food.

There were delegates present from the United States, from Austria, Germany, Switzerland, Holland, Poland and Belgium, not to mention those from all over India. From Nainital and Bhopal, from Bengal and Bihar, from Odisha and Andhra, devotees and disciples met and exchanged love and goodwill under the loving guidance of their teacher. Many old disciples of Gurudev, some of them yogacharyas, were happy to meet after a long time on this joyous occasion. Both the inaugural and the seminar were a memorable spiritual feast. I was fortunate to be present there.

During the ten-day festival, a typical day started at 7 a.m. with hundreds assembled in the meditation hall chanting *Om*. This was followed by invocations to the guru and guided meditation. After breakfast, the disciples spent some time in *seva,* which included different projects like cleaning the premises, and helping in the kitchen. At 11 a.m., the sessions started with devotional songs led by the guru as the assembled hundreds joined him in chorus. Following the ancient tradition of teaching through questions and answers, Baba enlightened his listeners on many spiritual truths with apt examples and interesting anecdotes, speaking with equal ease in English, Hindi and Odia and some Bengali and German. These sessions ended up being the most inspiring and stimulating discourses on Kriya Yoga, the Upanishads and world religion. The session ended with a brief meditation.

Then there was the evening session at 4 p.m., which was the highlight of the day. The evening program included a discourse by an invited speaker each day. Many renowned monks and other spiritual personalities spoke on the topics of *yoga, bhakti, karma,* and *vedanta,* blessing the audience with their presence and *satsang*. This was followed by guided meditation and the day's activities concluded with *prasad*.

During this period, Baba also was an invited speaker at several spiritual organizations and educational institutions, where he discoursed on spiritual life, kindling the light of knowledge in many young students as well as their teachers.

6

OPENING
CLOSED DOORS

In the year 2000, we decided to visit the various shrines and monuments of the Self Realization Fellowship established by Paramahamsa Yogananada. We reached Santa Monica, California at about 4 p.m. and checked into our hotel. We left almost immediately for the Lake Shrine and were a little disappointed to find it closed. Later we found out that all S.R.F. temples are closed on Mondays.

We spent a quiet evening on the beach watching the sunset over the Pacific. It was very peaceful. Gazing at the sun, the ocean, the mountains and the sky, we were reminded of Baba's words at one of his lectures. He had explained how these five elements were the visible manifestations of God in the outer universe, and are responsible for the five chakras in the inner universe.

Lake Shrine

The next morning we set out early, as we had to return to San Jose that same day. We went back to the Lake Shrine and roamed the gardens for some time, visiting the windmill chapel and the houseboat in which Paramahamsa Yogananada conducted services and spent long hours in meditation. It was thrilling to be treading the same grounds. It was past 9 a.m. and not finding

any signs of the upper shrine being opened, we asked one young man working in the garden, who called someone else to inquire. We were told they might not be able to open as they were understaffed, but would let us go up the stairs just to take a look from the outside. By then, a young visitor from India who had also come to pay his respects to Yoganandaji joined us.

I was praying to Yoganandaji, that we had come this far and to allow us to see the shrine. We went up to see what little we could but just as we turned around to come down, we heard someone open the door. The lady on the other side said the shrine was closed for the day but she would open it for us for a few minutes. We were very happy and sat inside. While there, I reflected on all that Paramahamsa Yogananda had accomplished in the West and how Baba was working now, day and night, along those same lines, reaching people and helping them to reach God. I realized gratefully that God sends his messengers from time to time to guide his children back on the right track.

Washington Memorial

We left the Lake Shrine to visit the Washington Memorial, which is considered the Mother Center. The young man from India expressed his wish to accompany us for the rest of the day. As we reached the Mother Center, a tour was just underway which we joined and were very happy to see the wishing well, where there were impressions of the hands and feet of the great master - the hands and feet that worked incessantly in the service of God. I was reminded of Baba again and Prajnana Mission, and prayed silently to Yogananadaji, "Here is another great soul, another Paramahamsa, walking in your footsteps, spreading the same message of Kriya. Let this mission be successful." We then visited the Temple of Leaves and after a short stop at the bookstore left to visit the Forest Lawn Cemetery to meditate at the crypt of Paramahamsa Yogananda.

A Magical Experience

All along the way, my husband was looking for a flower shop, feeling a great urge to offer flowers at the crypt. Fortunately, we found a flower shop at the entrance to the park and I went in to get some flowers. The young man with us also accompanied me. There were so many flowers of so many colors, that it was hard to choose. After some debating within myself as to what Yogananadaji would have liked, I was reminded of his devotion to the Divine Mother and decided to get a bouquet of red carnations, while our friend bought a bunch of white carnations. We continued our drive, and upon inquiring at the office for directions to the crypt, were asked to go to the next building.

"Look for a closed door," said the lady at the desk. "Ring the bell and some one will let you in." On our way there, my husband jokingly said, "Yoganandaji is really making us search for him." Also in humor, I replied, "That is not true. He opened many closed doors for us today," referring to the Lake Shrine. As we approached the next building, we were really amazed to find the door to the building wide open. There was no one in sight either outside or inside. The three of us went in and after locating the crypt, sat in front of it on a small bench. We noticed that there were already two flower arrangements on either side and interestingly enough they were also of red and white carnations. As we added our flowers, I thought it was a good decision, as the colors blended in.

We sat with closed eyes, but there were thoughts going through my mind about why people pray at burial places and if the presence of the departed soul would still be there, helping those who pray. We suddenly heard a sound like the opening of a gate and of something falling to the ground as if thrown from somewhere. We opened our eyes and on the floor in front of us, was a large pink rose, very fresh, like it was just plucked. There was no one in sight. We three were the only ones present in that whole building. We could not speak or move for some time. Finally my husband bent down and picked up the rose. The flower was remarkably heavy, very flat and had no stem at all. There were no roses anywhere in the room, and it was exactly like the roses we saw that morning at the Mother Center. It was like a blessing, and the joy we felt cannot be described. It was as though Yoganandaji had heard our prayers and assured us of his guidance. There was no other explanation. When we returned to San Jose, I called Baba and told him what happened. He said, "Be happy, it is a beautiful experience."

Moving to Kansas

We moved to Kansas at the end of 1999. My husband moved first in the month of November. I stayed behind in Cleveland for a few more months in order to sell our house. After five years in Cleveland as center leaders for the Cleveland area Kriya group, we had just settled down, and it was only an unexpected lay off and the search for a new job that landed us in Kansas. We were not too happy about moving, but since the plan was to retire in a couple of years anyway, we felt it did not matter as much and that I could continue my writing and editing work from anywhere. I was a little sad, as Kansas had no official Kriya Center and the chances of Baba coming to Kansas were almost none.

I went to Kansas for a visit in November, before officially moving there. Interestingly, the first person I met there was

Baba's Lecture Visit to Central Missouri University

Marla Selvidge, the wife of my husband's boss. Over dinner, I found out that Marla was the Professor and Director of the Department of Religious Studies at University of Central Missouri, and was very interested in Hindu religion. During the conversation, I mentioned Baba and his teachings, and she was immediately interested in having him visit the campus, talk to her students, and also give a public lecture at the campus.

I went to India in January and I mentioned our discussion to Baba while I was there. It was a year during which he had no travel plans in the United States, but he kindly agreed to visit. Marla was great at planning and organizing the event and between the two of us, we did all that we could. Since he was coming anyway, I looked into the possibility of lectures at the Hindu Temple also, and Marla suggested talking to the Unity School of Christianity. Both the temple and the church were very happy about having a great personage like him visiting the Kansas area.

The lecture at Unity Village had an audience of close to eight hundred people. It was a great event. Baba's talk about prayer and meditation was so inspiring that it was later published as a booklet.

University of Central Missouri had an exhibit about Hinduism arranged in the lobby of the new library building in his honor. The audiences were large and the response was tremendous and wherever he went, people loved him.

Though it was not a regular Kriya Yoga program, people were so inspired that many wanted initiations and Baba kindly agreed. We had about thirty initiations and with that the Kansas Kriya group was officially recognized.

Guru's Blessing at Shastipurti

Shashtipurti

In the month of March, 2000, Jyothi arranged a grand celebration for Harinath Baba's shashtipurti, sixtieth birthday. In Hindu culture, the sixtieth birthday is significant and a couple usually renews their vows at that time. We went to San Jose, where Jyothi was now living, and she arranged the ceremony and lunch at the Sunnyvale Temple. We invited and requested Baba to be present at this special occasion and he was kind enough to fly in from Vienna to spend three days with us. We were so blessed to have him present and to gain his blessings. The next day, nearly the entire extended family living in California was initiated into Kriya Yoga by Baba himself.

Each year, Baba's mission was progressing. With many projects in the Indian ashrams, it was becoming harder for him to travel to all the centers each year, so people from nearby cities started coming to locations where he had programs.

International Intensive Kriya Yoga Seminars

The International Seminar in India became an annual event. Our next visit was in the year 2001. This time the seminar was announced ahead of time, and was combined with some sightseeing trips to Kolkata. We were in charge of the arrangements for North America. About 20 delegates from the United States attended that year and Harinath took great care of the group in every possible way throughout the event. Many were first time visitors to India. In spite of some confusion in booking hotels, the disciples were very flexible and cooperative. Since the dorms at the ashram were still under construction, we all stayed at the seaside hotels, and buses transported us back and forth to the ashram.

Crossing Ganga for Dakshineswar

A couple of days before the retreat started, there was the inauguration of the Permanent Health Center at Balighai. The Shankaracharya of Puri, who also laid the foundation stone only six months before, was delighted to inaugurate the facility. Work on all fronts was progressing rapidly and it was getting more and more difficult to see or talk to Baba. But in his compassion, he never failed to greet anyone he was passing by with a kind word. I was still fortunate in the midst of all this to have a quick trip with Baba to see Lord Jagannath. The retreat was very successful as usual.

Pilgrimages

After the retreat, my husband and I, as well as a few other Indian disciples, had the privilege of going to Kumbhamela with Baba and the other monks of Prajnana Mission. Swami Mangalananda from Vienna also joined us. The Kumbhamela is a Hindu pilgrimage in which pilgrims gather to bathe in the sacred rivers and is held every three years at one of four holy sites, repeating in each place only once every twelve years. Each of the sites is believed to contain the sacred nectar that spilled from the pot as the gods carried it across the heavens.

This was our first experience of Kumbhamela. Accommodation was provided in one of the tents of the Shankaracharya of Puri, with whom the mission had a good relationship by now. He was very fond of Baba. It was a simple tent with a lot of straw on the ground covered with blankets and sheets, which served as bedding. One side was for men and the other side for women. There were bathrooms outside and a dining tent close by, where food was provided.

It was nice to stay in the company of the monks, to sit and listen to them talk. How we managed to bathe in the *sangam* on that day with that sea of humanity, God alone knows. Later we heard in the news that seven crore people took a dip in the *sangam* that day.

From Allahabad to Varanasi, we were unable to book reservations and were forced to travel in a luggage compartment with 50 – 60 people crowded inside, and with no toilet facilities, in freezing cold weather. Instead of the expected three hours, that train took almost six hours to reach Varanasi. When Baba heard the people around complaining and quarrelling for place, he started singing *bhajans*. The crowd became quiet instantly and he kept singing for almost six hours.

He was unwell with a sore throat and watery eyes due to dust allergies, but just kept going. By the time we finally arrived, no one was in a hurry in spite of the long journey. It was touching to see the villagers quickly collecting a *gurudakshina,* an offering to the guru of forty rupees among themselves and offer it to the monk who had ashrams all over the world. He accepted it with great humility, thanking them and giving them advice on simple spiritual *sadhana*. I will never forget that.

Kashi, City of Light

When we finally reached Varanasi, we found there were only three hours before our next train would leave for Calcutta. We decided to make a quick trip to see Lord Vishwanath of Varanasi. The holy city of Varanasi, also known as Benares or Kashi, is said to be the oldest surviving city in the world. According to legend, the first Siva *jyotirlingam,* the fiery pillar of light, came through the earth here and flared into the sky. Therefore Varanasi is also called Kasi, which means City of Light.

Lord Siva is known by the name Vishwanath here. The Sivalinga installed in the temple remains the devotional focus of Varanasi. Millions of pilgrims converge here to perform an *abhishekam* to the sacred *jyotirlingam* with the sacred water of river Ganga. The pilgrimage to Varanasi and the *darshan* of Lord Vishwanath is considered to be the most holy of pilgrimages by all Hindus.

The temple is said to be dear to Lord Siva. Hindus believe that those who die here attain liberation. Some also believe that the Lord resides here and is the giver of liberation and happiness. It is said that one who prays to and worships Vishwanath with devotion attains all his desires, and one who incessantly recites His name attains all *siddhis* or powers, and finally gains liberation.

We set out with Baba and a few others in auto rickshaws. When we got closer, we found that the road was blocked off to traffic and we had to walk about a mile to reach the temple. We had a quick *darshan* and while returning had trouble finding rickshaws. Luckily, we were able to get back to the train station just in time. We were very happy to have the *darshan* of the Lord even if it was a hurried trip. We reached Kolkata the next morning.

Dakshineswar

That evening we set out to visit the Dakshineswar Temple. The Dakshineswar Temple was built in 1855 by Rani Rashmoni, after she had a dream about the Divine Mother. The temple is three stories high with nine spires in the traditional Bengali style. In the sanctum sanctorum, there is a beautiful shining black idol of the Goddess Kali, her red tongue protruding and her right foot placed firmly on the chest of a prostrate Siva. She is known here as Bhavatarini and both idols are contained on a thousand-petalled silver lotus. Next to the main temple, there are twelve small Siva temples and in the same complex, there is a Radha Kanta temple.

We traveled to the temple in a small rowboat on the Ganga. Baba and Swami Shuddhananda sat on one corner of the boat and we sat on the other. There was a beautiful evening breeze and the sun was just setting in the muddied waters.

Once we were in the temple, the *darshan* of the very same Kali that Sri Ramakrishna worshipped and made famous, brought back many details that I had read about the great Master and the Divine Mother. The God intoxicated Master was a priest in the same Kali temple and he was so absorbed in his devotion, people at first thought he was mad. He experienced many divine visions of the Mother and is said to have had constant conversations with Her. Baba pointed to the different places - It was nice to see the room where the holy mother Sharada Devi stayed and cooked for the Master and his disciples. It was a nice trip again on the Ganga coming back to the city.

Jadavpur

On our return to the station, we had to leave right away to the place where Baba's lecture program was the next day, Jadavpur University. The lecture was arranged by Indumati Sabha Griha. Dr Ojah, a longtime disciple, was coordinating the program. We went to the quarters that were arranged for us, the ground floor of a building that had three rooms and a bathroom. Swami Mangalananda, Brahmacharinis Ambika and Usha, and I, were in one room. Baba, Shuddhanandaji, and Brahmanandaji shared another room, and Gopalji, Aroopanandaji and Harinath were in a third room. Arrangements were made for the food to be prepared and delivered and the food was very typical Bengali food, very tasty. For breakfast, we had fruits and *chuda* and *mudi* as they called it, puffed rice and spicy mixture. Baba subsisted mostly on fruits. It was a great and rare privilege to live in such close quarters with Baba.

The program started the next day. It was a two-day program with lectures, meditation and Q&A sessions. Shuddhanandaji conducted the program. Baba's talks were inspiring as usual. It was touching to see how hard Baba was working to revive the old forgotten and neglected Kriya Yoga that had once flourished in this part of Bengal. On the second day, arrangements were made to listen to Gurudev's message from Miami over the telephone. There were many long time disciples of Hariharanandaji who were very thrilled to hear his voice.

Harinath Baba left for Kansas directly from Kolkata, as he had no more vacation, while the rest of us returned to Cuttack. We spent a few days in Cuttack and Bhubaneswar, visiting schools and talking to the children, and organizing health programs at various schools. We visited the Pattamundai High School's Annual Day celebrations, where Baba addressed the school children and had lunch in the newly constructed library, which had been funded by Baba the previous year. After lunch, many of the high school students had a question and answer session with Baba, and from there we left for the inauguration of the Patita Pabana temple at Pattamundai, which had been renovated.

Prajnana Mission was a major supporter in the renovation of the temple. I had visited this temple with Baba the year before and it was just a small room with deities at the time. Now it was a full-fledged temple. The king of Puri himself, Gajapathi Maharaja, attended the inaugural.

Returning to S.R.F. with Baba

Swami Shuddhanandaji, Brahmanandaji, and Arupanandaji were in the United States in the month of May to attend Gurudev's birthday. During the early part of May, Baba had a program in Los Angeles and he decided to take the swamis with him so they could visit the Self Realization Fellowship Centers. Despite our previous highly rewarding trip, we could not pass up this opportunity to visit again in Baba's company. I was always struck by the similarities between Baba and Yogananda, and the striking parallels between their missions in the West.

We arrived in L.A. at almost midnight, and renting a car, drove to the home of our host, who was a good friend and a former colleague of Harinath. By the time we reached his home, Sheila Ma, at whose house Baba was staying, had already called twice to enquire about our arrival.

Early the next morning, we talked to Sheila, and getting directions, we set out for their house in Beverly Hills, which afforded a fantastic view of both the Pacific Ocean and Los Angeles. When we rang the bell, Baba himself opened the door and we went in after bowing to him. It was nice to see all the swamis together and Baba in charge of his group. Sheila Ma, a very gracious host, offered us breakfast along with the swamis and asked if we could escort the swamis on that day, as both she and her husband were on call. It was more than we could hope for – to spend the whole day in the holy company, visiting the sacred places of Paramahamsa Yoganandaji.

We once again visited the Washington Memorial, the tomb of Yoganandaji, the Hollywood Temple and the Lake Shrine. Everywhere we went, the welcome was unusually warm and loving. The S.R.F. residents even arranged for one of their brahmacharis to accompany us and show us around. It was a beautiful and inspiring experience. At the Washington Memorial, we saw Yoganandaji's handprints embedded in the concrete near the wishing well. There were also many of the pink roses that they said he was fond of, and I could not help but remember our experience from the year before, when we had visited the tomb.

At the Lake Shrine, walking the grounds with Baba was exhilarating. We saw the boat on which Yoganandaji meditated sometimes and the windmill. Then we went up to see the meditation hall. The doors were again especially opened for us. We sat for a few minutes and meditated. As I sat there, I was thinking what a great opportunity it was to sit there and meditate in the presence of Baba. It occurred to me that Baba would now have the task of propagating the great Kriya lineage from which both he and Yogananda had descended. On the way back, we talked about the projects of Prajnana Mission both in India and abroad. We returned to Sheila Ma's house late in the evening. We had dinner there and stayed as long as we could, before returning to our host.

San Diego

The next morning we went to San Diego to visit Yoganandaji's home. We went in two cars since Baba's hosts had both taken the day off to accompany the swamis. On our way there, Baba and Arupanandaji went in Uttam Baba's car and Shuddhanandaji and Brahmanandaji came with us. We went to Encinitas. The rolling gardens with the view of the Pacific were extremely beautiful and it was a wonderful place to sit and meditate. We had to wait until 4 p.m. for someone to open the residence of Yoganandaji, but it was worth the wait. We meditated there for sometime.

Hidden Valley

We then set out for the Hidden Valley retreat. True to its name, Hidden Valley was really tucked away. We drove for miles and miles and all of a sudden came upon this beautiful place. There we met the most loving elderly swami by the name of Vimalananda, who had known Yoganandaji during his lifetime. He was an American swami but had the most striking resemblance to my father. Baba did not give his identity and we introduced ourselves as disciples of the swamis visiting from India. But somehow Vimalananda must have felt some bond and took an instant liking to Baba and our group. He escorted us through the gardens of the grounds, and to a most amazing collection of hibiscus plants.

The colors and the sizes of the flowers were beyond imagination and this swami walked us through thousands of the blooms, stopping here and there to present us with an unusual specimen. By the time we were done, we all ended up with plenty of flowers in our hands and took some really good photographs.

We continued our walk and Baba discovered some edible fruit on the trees. We sat under the trees for a while and the residents lovingly served us some apple juice. Finally, it was time to leave and Baba gave all the residents a loving hug. Deeply moved by the love and humility of Vimalananda, Baba prostrated to him under the pretext of showing him how people bow in India. At that point I do not know what moved me, but tears started flowing down my face so profusely that all attempts to stop them were of no use. I cried to my heart's content and felt really cleansed. It may have been something about the love of the old swami and his resemblance to my father.

We said our goodbyes and headed toward the cars, when Baba as a last minute surprise got into our car with Arupanandaji and the others went in Uttam Baba's car. As the car started moving, Baba, as though to cheer me up, said lovingly, "See, I switched cars." I smiled through my tears and said, "Yes, Baba, I see it." The next day the swamis were leaving for the program in Santa Barbara. After breakfast, we said goodbye and headed back to Kansas.

It was a great trip. It was a privilege and an honor to visit these places in the company of these monks from the same Kriya lineage as Paramahamsa Yogananda. We were surprised at how much Yoganandaji had achieved single-handedly and how many hearts he had won. Baba said that he wanted us to see how much could be done by a person with firm determination and faith in God. I was equally touched by Baba's dedication and the kind of love Baba evoked wherever he went. It was another memorable visit.

Navaratri in Kansas

We were fortunate to have Baba visit Kansas as well that year, and stay with us. This was extra special as it was during Navaratri time. We had *chandi havan* for the 7th, 8th and 9th days of the festival. Often, Baba is like a loving mother to his disciples, transforming them with his love and example rather than with rules and imposed discipline. He would come to the *puja* room each morning and evening during the *arati* time. It was like the Divine Mother stayed with us all those days and we thanked the Mother who blessed us with this holy presence. It felt like Her response for the many years of our attempts to reach Her.

We had lectures again at two of the Unity Churches and also at the Hindu Temple. The program was a great success and rather hectic as it was also a regular Kriya program with initiations and guided meditations. People from several other states attended the program.

Jyothi brought her fiance Ramesh to meet Baba and he immediately asked to be initiated. Jyothi also received her second Kriya initiation at this time. How Baba had the strength and energy to do so much work with such great love and a smile on his face, God only knows. Not only did he work, he also became a source of energy for others and radiated so much love that no one else felt the least bit tired or wanted to leave his presence.

A Special Birthday with Gurudev

In the year 2001, we wanted to attend Gurudev's birthday in Miami. Though we made trips to Miami whenever Baba was present there, we had never attended Gurudev's birthday. On my last trip to India, I had purchased a turban in Hyderabad. It was a beautiful turban made of beige and gold fabric lined with strings of pearls on one side and with a diadem in the center. It looked very regal. Along with it, I also bought a scarf of the same color and a pearl garland, which we wanted to present to Gurudev. We were not sure if he would wear them, but took them along with us to Miami. We reached Miami on the 26th of May and we talked to Baba about presenting our gifts to Gurudev the next day. Baba looked at them and said, "They are nice, but it depends on Gurudev whether he will wear them. You can present them and see."

Gurudev tired easily in those days. After his shower and when he was dressed, Gurudev was resting on his bed wrapped in a red shawl. The monks and some close disciples were assembled by his bedside, and we went in with the shawl and the turban and the garland neatly arranged on a tray and sat down.

Baba and Shuddhanandaji started singing. This was customary on each birthday. Gurudev loved music and listening to songs. He would also join in singing some of his favorites. Many yogacharyas and people from many countries came for this birthday. The singing continued for three hours, during which disciples came in and bowed to Gurudev's feet.

After Gurudev rested sufficiently, it was time to go to the hall, where disciples were waiting for the celebration. Baba and Shuddhanandaji helped him to get up from the bed and Gurudev glanced at the things on the tray and smiled. Baba humbly requested him to wear them and ventured to put the shawl on him and slowly the head dress. Gurudev really looked like a Maharaj, an emperor, in that attire. They held a mirror in front of him so he could see himself, and Gurudev was smiling. We were so happy that he did wear them.

As Gurudev was tired and weak, they took off the heavy turban and walked him to the hall. In the meantime I wanted to make a garland for him. There were many roses that people brought and I asked someone if I could quickly make a rose garland. They said I could, but were not sure if he would be comfortable wearing a heavy rose garland. I decided to make one anyway and arranging it on a tray, left it on the dais where Gurudev was seated. Gurudev came and sat down. He sent Baba back to get his turban and had it again put on his head. He then pointed to the rose garland and someone put it around his neck. Weak as he was, I knew that he was doing it for the benefit of the disciples who wished to see him in that attire, and I thought how compassionate a guru is to fulfill the wish of the children, even if it was not convenient for him. During that birthday, Gurudev made a profound statement. He said, "It is not a function we celebrate, we celebrate the functioning of God within us."

I reflected on how true that is. All the celebrations, birthdays, graduations, weddings, anniversaries that we celebrate, what are they? Would they be possible if God was not breathing through us day and night? If He did not function, then what function could we celebrate? The whole purpose of life is to discover that divine joy in the heart and mind and bring inner fulfillment.

Visiting Yuktashram

On my trip to India, I also had the chance to visit Yuktashram in Bishindipur. Bishindipur is a remote village in West Bengal. One can get there by taking a train to Kharagpur, and then traveling an hour by road, or from Howrah to Balichak in a local train and the rest of the trip by car. The journey takes you through the most beautiful countryside full of fertile paddy fields, lush coconut trees and banana groves. It is unpolluted, and indescribably serene.

The ashram itself is located on a fifteen-acre tropical paradise. Known as Yuktashram, it is around sixty years old. Upon arrival, one sees a beautiful three-storied building, which stands in contrast to the surrounding rural area of small cottages. It was originally a compact building with a small meditation room, two tiny bedrooms and a verandah leading to the dining area. Now it has been expanded to add another two floors, the first floor housing three bedrooms with attached bathrooms with modern amenities, and the second floor with two extra bedrooms.

Behind the ashram lie vast stretches of paddy and mustard fields. The acres of beautiful yellow flowers from the mustard-seed crop and the emerald green of the paddy fields are quite spectacular. Peanuts and lentils are also grown at the ashram. The ashram has a beautiful garden with many varieties of fruits and flowers. There is also a vegetable patch that grows vegetables in season. Many unusual trees and plants surround the building itself. There is an old jackfruit tree, which Shuddhanandaji explained has been there from Gurudev's time in India. There are cinnamon, bay leaves, clove, cardamom and turmeric plants. Raw turmeric is soft and edible, and is supposed to be good for the health. There is also a picturesque pond, lined with many trees.

The ashram came into existence through the combined efforts of Swami Narayan Giri and Paramahamsa Hariharananda, and was named Yuktashram in memory of their beloved guru, Shriyukteshwar. What started out as a small house, turned into a beautiful hermitage in a secluded place. Shriyukteshwar Vidyayatan, a school for children, was also started at that time and is still running.

This remote ashram is managed through the excellent supervision of Swami Shuddhananda with the cooperation of some very sincere disciples. It was a unique experience to walk through the fields and around the ashram grounds while Shuddhanandaji explained its history, and described the nature of the crops and the trees that make the ashram self-sufficient.

Nothing needs to be bought from outside, except salt. There are seven cows that yield plenty of milk. There is an abundance of grain, vegetables, fruits, flowers and dairy products; even the cooking gas is produced on the premises from cow dung.

The place is extraordinarily quiet and only birds and insects interrupt the silence. It is peaceful, secluded and beautiful, an ideal place for one who wants to be apart from the world, and engage in spiritual practice. No regular programs are conducted, unless the monks are there. At that time, the village folks come to pay their respects, and to meditate.

On this trip, during Baba's brief stay, the children from the ashram school came to visit, and he gave them advice on student life and discipline. The children had prepared a program of song and dance, and left after receiving sweets as *prasad*. Baba has a unique way of interacting with children, which I observed at the many schools he visited. He becomes one among the children, and instantly puts them at ease by asking them questions and letting them speak instead of giving them a lecture. Through the dialogue that ensues, he nevertheless manages to make them see what is right. In the evening there was a *satsang* for the adults. A ninety-year-old devotee sang to the Divine Mother in the most moving and beautiful way. Then everyone had *prasad*.

The dedicated brahmacharis that work in the ashram are very loving and sincere, performing their duties throughout the year, waiting in anticipation of the few days spent in the holy company of the Kriya monks. Love is the guiding force at Yuktashram – Paramahamsa Prajnananada's love for his brother monks, brahmacharis, and disciples and for humanity at large is evident, as well as the tremendous love he receives from them in return.

At the time of my visit, plans were underway for building a large meditation hall, since the kitchen and the dining hall had just been completed. Construction had also begun for a small dispensary to serve the needy. The trip to Yuktashram was memorable. It is an ideal place for those who want to meditate and do *sadhana* in seclusion.

7

MAHASAMADHI OF GURUDEV

In 2002, I went to India to attend the January program at Hariharananda Gurukulam. As I always did, I went to Hyderabad first, to visit my parents and mother-in-law. I was getting ready to leave for Odisha to attend the Intensive International Kriya Yoga Seminar that started from the 14th. I usually arrived a few days early to attend the Gita talks as well, but this time I faced a few problems, first the India trip had to be postponed, then I lost a day in Amsterdam due to a flight cancellation and by the time I arrived in Hyderabad on the 8th, I heard that my flight to Bhubaneswar had been postponed to the 10th of January.

I called Baba on the 9th and was about to explain, when he said in a very calm voice, "It has been a hectic day. I am just coming back after the Gita talk in Bhubaneswar. You know, something happened yesterday. The father of Prajnanananda passed away." I could not speak for a few moments and then said, "Baba, I am so sorry to hear this."

I left Hyderabad the next day on the 6 a.m. flight to Bhubaneshwar, happy that I would at least be able to attend the Gita talk in Cuttack. As luck would have it, the plane could not land due to dense fog and ended up being rerouted to Kolkata. It was a big disappointment as I was anxious to get there. We had to spend a long time in the Kolkata airport, as there was no flight again till the evening. Luckily, Pratima Ma, a disciple from Bhubaneswar who traveled with me from Hyderabad was there to keep me company, and we were both glad about that.

We finally reached Bhubaneshwar at 5:45 p.m. Pratima Ma's son, who came to pick her up, brought an extra car with a driver who could take me straight to Cuttack so I could attend Baba's talk that evening. I stopped at Vidyasagar Baba's house on the way, and he and another disciple came with me to the Town Center in Cuttack. When we arrived there, the program had started and Vidyasagar Baba escorted me to a seat in the front row that was vacant. I was surprised to see Rabinarayan Baba giving an introductory talk and Baba sitting with his eyes closed in meditation right in front of me. It was such a great feeling to see him that in spite of the long trip and all the waiting, I felt completely refreshed.

I have been fortunate enough to see him like that many times before, during other talks and introductions. But that is immaterial. Whenever I see him in that pose, with a radiant countenance and light emanating out to a large area around him, the experience is quite unique. Often it would occur to me that all he needed to do was close his eyes and lift those eyebrows and he could enter into instant communion with the Divine. I felt so exhilarated and filled with energy, my whole body quivered, tears streamed down my face and that familiar feeling of "I am home. I don't need anything else," filled me with happiness.

Finally, Baba started speaking. Even as he started the introductory prayer, the audience was spellbound. He elevates and transforms a gathering instantly with his own simple style of explaining great truths in sweet, precise words. The lecture was an introduction to the Gita in Odia. The beauty and the richness of his language struck me. I did not know much of the language, but have never failed to understand his lectures in Odia. I have listened to the same lectures in English, but what a difference the language could make was evident.

Baba's Odia was fluent and high-flown and was a stream of devotion, love and wisdom. He combined the love of a mother and the discipline of a father, gently prodding the audience to examine themselves, to improve, to progress, to turn Godward and to be aware of the goal. The seemingly simple speech was filled with so many precious teachings for those who had the ears to listen. It was not a lecture. It was the call of the Divine to wake up the masses.

Baba concluded with a comment. "How many of you really want God and really want to listen to his song with a desire to change yourself? If you do, congratulations. If not, please make an attempt from this very moment." The first day of the Gita discourses was concluded with a chorus of devotional singing. I made a renewed resolve to apply the Gita's teachings in my own life.

Demise of Baba's Father

About 11 p.m. that night, Baba finally left for Pattamundai to visit his bereaved mother, as he had no time during the day. When I had the chance to speak with Baba the next day, I asked him about how his father had died and whether he was able to see him before he passed away.

According to Baba, his father Shri Niranjan Dash had been in the hospital. He had been suffering from severe asthma attacks for a while and was on oxygen support. Before Baba arrived in Cuttack, his father had informed everyone that he was waiting for Baba's arrival and would leave his body only after seeing him. Baba's parents were both initiated into Kriya Yoga by Gurudev at Karar Ashram in the year 1984.

Upon his arrival, Baba was informed of his father's condition and was able to be at his bedside for a short time. His father felt blessed and expressed his happiness and asked his son to go back to his program and not waste time. Baba went back to Bhubaneswar for the evening public address there, which was attended by hundreds of people. The next day was the dedication ceremony of the new ambulance for the Health Center at the Balighai Clinic, followed by the groundbreaking ceremony for a library at the Beleswar College. Sri Shankaracharya of Puri was the chief guest at both occasions and the programs were conducted as scheduled.

At 1:40 p.m., the news arrived that Shri Niranjan Dash had left his body, chanting the name of God in his last moments. In the Gita, the Lord says, "One who leaves the body remembering me even in his last moments will attain Me, there is no doubt in this." Niranjan Dash was able to fulfill both the wish to see his son at his bedside before his departure and the chanting of God's name in his final moments.

Under Baba's directions, the cremation was performed at Svargadvar, which means Gateway to Heaven, in the sacred land of Jagannath. Thus ended a chapter in the life of Baba, with the loss of his physical father. It is surprising that in spite of a hectic schedule around the globe, it was possible by the grace of God for him to fulfill his father's wish to be at his bedside. I am reminded of Shri Shankaracharya who did the same for his mother. God watches out for those who really depend on Him.

The program went on undisturbed. The same evening, Baba continued with the Bhubaneshwar lectures, again attended by thousands of enthusiastic aspirants. We have read about Lahiri Mahashaya discoursing on the Gita as the dead body of his daughter lay in the next room. Here was another example of one who practiced what he preached. These are true Sthita Prajnas, those who continue in the performance of their duties, unfazed by life's gains and losses. I felt blessed to have come into contact with one of them.

The Residential Brahmachari Training Program

In 2002, Baba planned the first Residential Brahmachari Training Program. The ashram was expanding and we needed more brahmacharis and brahmacharinis to carry on the work of Gurudev. In May 2001, we visited the ashram in Miami just before Gurudev's birthday. Noticing a pile of notebooks by Baba's desk, I asked what they were. Baba showed me the handwritten notes of the syllabus and curriculum for the planned brahmachari training course that was to begin in June. Even while traveling from center to center each week conducting Kriya programs and retreats and writing books, Baba still found time to plan the brahmachari training courses.

The central theme of the Residential Brahmachari Training Course (RBTC) is to select people of diverse nationalities, races, religions, and gender to participate in the course and prepare them to live a wholesome and integrated life through the practice of discipline, meditation, and moderation. The residential courses are offered free of cost and are beneficial for people of all faiths.

They offer an opportunity to live a conscious life and resist and transform the increasing challenges and difficulties of modern society through love and tolerance.

The first training course was held with forty selected trainees for three months under Baba's guidance. He worked with us starting with the exercise class from 4.30 a.m. through most of the day teaching the course material, leading chanting classes, and guiding meditations. I was fortunate enough to be allowed to attend the course as a participant. It was a tough training course with the day starting at 4 a.m. in the morning and ending at 10 p.m. In spite of the summer heat and power cuts, the three-month course was completed successfully.

The scope and the syllabus of the course covered an outline of the basic philosophies of the East and the West, a basic understanding of Sanskrit, an elaborate study of the Bhagavad Gita as a practical guide for spiritual life, with reference to the Upanishads, the Bible, the Patanjali Yoga Sutras, and other yogic scriptures and vedantic texts. On the practical side, there were explanations of Kriya Yoga meditation, discourses, group discussions and question and answer sessions. It was a great learning experience.

At the end of the training, an opportunity for apprenticeship is offered to candidates interested in serving the ashrams. Successful candidates are then initiated and become the brahmacharis and brahmacharinis of the lineage. From those selected candidates, some are initiated into monkhood when the guru considers them as ready.

I attended most of the training courses as a participant. The four-month course that focused on the Bhagavad Gita, with 365 hours of solid instruction, was a spiritual wonder. Baba would teach classes for a three-hour stretch and once he took his seat and started, there was no concept of time. Very often it felt like the class ended too soon. The whole class transformed into one Arjuna listening intently to Baba, who guided us like Lord Krishna.

In 2002, we also had the chance to see the Chariot festival of Lord Jagannath. Prajnana Mission organized a bookstore, a health camp and a first aid center in Puri to assist the chariot festival pilgrims. The brahmacharis from the ashram took turns serving in these facilities.

Baba was serving on all fronts. During this time, Prajnana Mission also provided housing for flood victims. Baba presided over the event. The King of Puri and other monks were also present. I was happy to be there to see this great charitable event where keys for new homes were given to those who were affected.

Gurudev's Mahasamadhi

We were hearing reports on and off that Gurudev was not well and in November, we decided we would visit him, even if it was for a couple of days. Baba was in London at the time. I called him in London and told him of our intended visit, and Baba said, "Visit him and let me know how he is."

We went to Homestead and found that Gurudev was no longer coming out of his room, and people were not allowed to go into his room. Efforts to get him out of his room were unsuccessful, as he refused to come out. Swami Shuddhananda was there and Angie Ma and Katharine Ma were also there. We were very disappointed at not being able to at least see him from the door of his room. We had to leave the day after and I was praying really hard that we should be able to somehow see him.

The next day at lunchtime, Katharine Ma said, "If you want to go in now, do it quickly, but don't stay long." We were overjoyed to be able to have *darshan* and went in along with Shuddhanandaji. We sat on our knees near his bed. Gurudev very lovingly held our hands and asked, "From where have you come?" When we said Kansas, he repeated the word Kansas a couple of times, and kept saying he was very happy. We were about to get up to leave remembering that we should not disturb him for long, but at that moment Gurudev clasped our hands and wouldn't let go. We slowly got up and came out after bowing at his feet. I was very happy to have this opportunity.

The Last Garden Visit

Then at 4 p.m. that evening, Gurudev miraculously agreed to come out. Wrapped in a red shawl and with a red vermilion mark shining on his forehead, Gurudev was wheeled out of his room by Shuddhanandaji. The few people who were there followed him into the garden. The meditation hall was not complete at the time and he had to be wheeled out through the hall into the garden.

As we passed through the banana groves, someone pointed out a bunch of ripe bananas, and Gurudev asked that it be cut and the bananas given out as *prasad*. As we continued further he grew tired, and his head began tilting to one side, so Shuddhanandaji brought him back to the room. We came back with a heavy heart –it was painful to see him like that. It was to be Gurudev's last garden tour.

As his condition deteriorated and Gurudev began asking for him, Baba was called back from London. Gurudev was admitted to the hospital and after eight days in the hospital, he attained *mahasamadhi* on December 3rd. By then Brahmanandaji had also arrived from India. Baba stayed with Gurudev day and night for those eight days.

Baba's Message

On the evening of December 7th, for the first time after the Mahasamadhi of Gurudev, Baba addressed the small gathering present at the Miami center in a tearful voice and shared with us what transpired during that time.

Gurudev was admitted to the hospital on the 25th of November. In the hospital there was one verse, which he was always repeating.

Tvameva mata ca pita tvameva......

You are my mother, father, relative and, friend. You are my everything. Oh God, I bow to you.

Gurudev also asked me "Can you sing a song for me? Write the song down for me so I can sing with you." It was the song of Rabindranath Tagore. We sang together.

"O God! Glory to Thee. Because of the life you gave, I live in this body. You have kept me in the arms of the Father and the lap of the Mother. You created the bond of Love between friends... Glory to Thee! O God."

The day before he left his body, he kept repeating, "O Almighty Father, Reveal Thyself just now." Gurudev asked me, "Did you finish all your work? I have finished all my work. Let us go." On that morning he said, "I bow to you unlimited times." The doctor said to me, "He is preparing himself. It could be very soon."

On December 3rd, at 6:48 p.m., we were all chanting the Gayatri Mantra. His breath was becoming slow. He left his body. From that time I don't know what has happened to me. I was not the same as I was a minute before.

We all are his successors to inherit his spiritual treasure through practice, love and inner prayer. In my life, I have served and followed him till today, and I will serve him to my last breath.

In all my time with him, he has not said a single word that caused me pain. He said, "You and I are inseparable. You cannot be without me and I cannot be without you."

Guru's love, guru's care, guru's compassion, guru's discipline and guru's training are all unique. True love is experienced in separation. We realize the value of someone or something when we are away from it.

That light that was in the physical frame will burn in the hearts of all, igniting love and wisdom within each of us. All of us have lived with Gurudev and experienced many things in our life. This is a great loss for all and also to my personal life. Spiritually what we are is because of Gurudev. No words can give solace and comfort to our mind and heart. I am not in a state to give a talk. At the suggestion of a loving disciple, I am spending a few minutes to tell you what happened during the last few days.

Baba at the Original Samadhi Mandir

Sri Guru Mandir

After sharing this poignant speech, Baba made all arrangements for the body to be flown to Balighai Ashram and was there to receive the body when it arrived. Gurudev's body arrived at the ashram on December 14th. *Darshan* was arranged and thousands of people came to pay tribute over the next two days. Finally the body was buried according to monastic rites on the site of the future samadhi mandir. Baba maintained a fast from the time Gurudev left his body till he was laid to rest, and all ceremonies were performed as per Hindu tradition. The death of his guru was a great loss to Baba.

Guru Mandir

Gurudev's body was laid to rest and a small *samadhi* shrine was built over it. Baba had the wish to build a beautiful shrine for Gurudev. It would not be just a samadhi mandir but a Guru Mandir, which would honor all gurus of the lineage, with Gurudev as the central figure. Baba wanted this monument to be completed in time for the centenary celebrations, to be held in 2007-2008.

Whenever I thought of Baba, Vivekananda came to mind. Gurudev was like Ramakrishna Paramahamsa, and Baba was the teacher like Vivekananda, who spread the Master's gospel. He had the same kind of will that Vivekananda spoke about- "gigantic wills which nothing can resist, which can penetrate into the mysteries and the secrets of the universe and accomplish their purpose, even if it meant meeting death face to face." (Vivekananda, 1897)

Everything that was accomplished by Prajnana Mission, monumental tasks in record time which an ordinary person would deem impossible, were a reflection of this willpower or *iccha shakti* which was also accompanied by *kriya shakti*, immediate action, and of course combined with wisdom or *jnana shakti*. The motivating power of Baba was his love. People competed to do his work and considered themselves blessed even if they could offer him a glass of water.

I remember when the construction of the Guru Mandir was being planned. I recall the small structure that was built just as a symbol over the *samadhi*. Before the construction, I had the opportunity to walk over to it with Baba and a couple of others. He went in and prayed near the *samadhi* and walked away to sit on a small mound at the back under a tree. None of us dared to follow him. He sat for a short time gazing at the small *mandir* and into the horizon and then got up and walked over to us. Walking back to the main building, on the way he said, "Do you know what it would cost to build the new Guru Mandir that we are planning?" When I guessed an amount, he smiled and said "No, much, much more." Then he added "Why can't it be done? Anything can be done for someone we love and who has given us so much." The words sounded like a prophecy.

Later, as the construction was progressing and reaching completion, I remember talking to the architect, who said, " In the beginning I used to encourage, and Baba used to hesitate, but now at the rate at which it is going, he is more confident than me." The building was completed as per schedule in time for the centenary celebrations in Puri.

The Guru Mandir turned out to be a masterpiece of architecture- an octagonal building that enshrined the gurus of the lineage, with a lifelike statue of Gurudev in the center. The huge area around the sanctum sanctorum could seat hundreds of people. The building was surrounded by gardens on all eight sides along with ponds filled with beautiful lotuses and water lilies. A very beautiful place full of powerful vibrations, it became a great place for meditation.

8

A Taste of
Ashram Life

Our daughter Jyothi married Ramesh in November of 2003. We were so happy that she had finally found the right person and welcomed Ramesh into our family. He was a very talented musician and had a kind and loving heart. He was also a wonderful father to our grandson Nikhil, who needed a father figure at the time. We all went to India together in December after their marriage. Our son Murali and his wife Jori also joined us on the trip. We held a reception in Hyderabad for both couples and invited our family and friends.

Programs in Bangalore and Hyderabad

Our youngest son Srinath was working for Intel in Bangalore during that period. Since I knew that Baba, along with Swami Brahmananda Giri and Swami Shuddhananda Giri, was scheduled to be in Bangalore, Mysore and Hyderabad for Kriya Yoga programs the following month, I stayed on in India with Srinath in Bangalore.

Bangalore Program

Baba and his monks were welcomed everywhere in the traditional manner for receiving men of God. It was a beautiful and divine experience to see how they were received in different places accompanied by the powerful chanting of Vedic mantras with great love and devotion.

Devotees in Bangalore formed a Prajnana Mission Welcome Committee that organized spiritual discourses on various topics in different places. Baba inspired and enlightened the audiences with his unique and soul-stirring lectures. He answered questions following the lectures with great love and patience, which further helped to clear disciples' doubts and quench their spiritual thirst.

In addition to the talks on the Bhagavad Gita and Kriya Yoga at the Bharatiya Vidya Bhavan and the Town hall of Bangalore, there were also sponsored talks at the reputed Indian Institute of Sciences and the Indian Institute of Management. Talking on the relevance of spirituality in the scientific era at the Institute of Sciences, Baba elaborated on how the mystic and the physicist arrive at the same conclusion - the essential unity of all things. While one started from the inner world and the other from the outer world, he noted how both the higher science and knowledge, and ordinary science and knowledge, have to both be investigated for human fulfillment.

In his message at the Institute of Management, Baba stressed the importance of choosing the right goals and making the right investments to realize the truth. The real goal is within, he said, and one should have the physical, mental and spiritual strength to pursue the goal to make life complete.

The Kriyavans at Mysore also provided a hearty welcome of love and devotion, and a lecture and group meditation were conducted there. During this visit we also had an opportunity to visit the Chamundeshwari Temple and Sravanabelagola.

Chamundeshwari temple sits on the top of a hill about 13 km from Mysore. The *gopura* or dome of the temple has intricate carvings. The deity Chamunda or Durga is a beautiful statue of the Divine Mother in all Her glory, and is rumored to be made out of gold. We made it there right before the temple was about to close and managed to have a beautiful visit. We also visited huge granite Nandi decorated with exquisite bells around its neck which sat in front of a Siva temple which is a short distance away.

Sravanabelagola is a famous Jain pilgrim site, also located on a hill. One has to climb about 600 steps to reach the summit and see the great statue of Sri Gomatheswar also known as Bahubali. The statue, which is over 58 feet high, is believed to be one of the tallest statues in the world, and is carved entirely out of granite.

At our request, Baba along with Brahmanandaji and Shuddhanandaji had dinner with us and stayed at Srinath's place the night before leaving for Hyderabad.

Hyderabad

Hyderabad was another story. The grand welcome and the reception for Prajnana Mission and Kriya Yoga with colorful banners and posters on all main streets reflected the great love of the Kriyavans. The devotion and dedication of the organizers resulted in a three-day Gita Discourse at the Bharatiya Vidya Bhavan, where packed audiences listened with rapt attention to Baba's talks. The question answer sessions were the highlight of the programs. He had a spontaneous answer for every question asked, and answered the shower of questions with limitless patience.

There were also talks at educational institutions. I introduced Baba to the assembled staff and students at Osmania University in Hyderabad. I was especially inspired as it was the college where I had studied, and also where I worked as a lecturer before we left for the United States.

In his lecture, Baba advised the staff and students to uphold their great tradition and culture and not to give in to blind imitation. Education is not complete without the study and practice of moral conduct and values, was his message. Students are the future of the country, he said, and asked them to set an example to others by living a life based on values. It was a pleasure to see the inspired students gather around Baba afterwards to pay their respects in the traditional way of touching the feet. Several of them lined up for autographs.

R.B.V.R.R College for Women sponsored and hosted a public discourse, in connection with their Silver Jubilee Celebrations. Hundreds of students and others listened to the talk "Yoga for the Body, Mind and Soul." Baba described how to keep the body and mind fit through proper exercise and diet and through good company. He elaborated on how brainpower, memory, and efficiency can all be enhanced, by practicing simple techniques of yoga and living a goal oriented life. This was yet another college where I had studied for a year and also worked as a lecturer for a year before I went on to Osmania University. It was nice to be back on the campus with Baba.

Initiations and guided meditations were conducted by the swamis in both Bangalore and Hyderabad, and were attended by hundreds of new disciples. Plans were made to conduct guided meditations at both places in the future.

The entire mission was one of love. Many hearts were conquered and lives were transformed by Baba, who put everything aside to help us walk on the path to God. At the end of the programs, the farewells were difficult. It was hard to part with that divine loving presence and the spiritual magnetism of the monks. Hearts were full and eyes were moist as Baba continued on his endless journey to awaken more spirits.

Miami Ashram

In April of 2004, I left for Miami, this time at the request of Katharine. She asked me to come spend time and help out with the transcribing of Gurudev's tapes for the centenary celebrations. I thought I would give it a try and see how ashram life in Miami would be. The flight was one hour late in arriving, but a couple of brahmacharis from the ashram met me at the airport. I reached the ashram around 5 p.m. right before dinner. After dinner, there was Gita study at 6:15 p.m, followed by meditation at 7 p.m.

The ashram atmosphere was impressive, nice and quiet. There were a few people taking care of the ashram and each of them was sincere, hard working and dedicated. It was good to see no conflicts or confusion and only love reflected in every one. The transformation that Baba brought about within a short time of his becoming the president of the organization was evident. People now had one teacher to look up to – one who loved them and guided them.

Just before lunch the next day, it was announced that Baba would be giving his weekly message and conference call to the ashramites over the telephone. This usually happened on Thursdays we were told, but since he was traveling, it would be on Friday this time. We all gathered around the phone in the office.

Then the talk began. I wish I had a paper and pen in hand to write down each of those words. They were so loving and beautiful. I wondered how one could convey that much love in a voice that came from so many miles away.

"To whom shall I talk?" he asked. "I am talking to myself, perceiving myself in you all. I am in all of you, and you are all in me. It is an inseparable existence and that is the truth." The conviction in that voice brought tears to my eyes. "People who are staying in the ashram taking care of Gurudev's home, it is a great opportunity for you to stay in that beautiful protected environment of the ashram and to serve the guru and do your own individual *sadhana*. Do not waste any time and make use of the opportunity." I finally understood how the residents kept going about their work with such dedication. A talk like that even once a week could keep you working forever. That was the reward, the genuine love of the teacher, a child of God who meant every word he said.

The weather was great in Miami and the grounds were beautiful. But by this point, the more I traveled, the more I felt it was not necessary. I felt the guru's presence with me all the time. But of course, the occasional physical presence definitely helped and inspired.

Baba was at the Miami ashram for the Easter program. He reached the ashram around 1:30 p.m. I was the first one to bow. It felt strange to be an ashramite receiving Baba in his ashram. I did not utter a word. I did not feel like talking. My eyes filled with tears. I asked myself, "Why? What do I want from him? Why do I feel down?" I decided to get over it. I went to the library and found a book by Swami Sivananda. I went and sat by the pond and read a chapter and meditated for some time and felt better. I reminded myself that I had to conquer expectation and feel the guru's presence all the time. There was no other way. Everything was inside. If you were really tuned in, you could communicate. See God in all and all in God- that was the lesson to be learned. It was easier said than done, however. Removing our defects is the real *sadhana* –other things are easy. The Easter program and retreat with Baba were very inspiring. I returned home after the program.

Balashram- A Dream Realized

Besides everything else, Baba was also a great believer in the power of education. He always had the vision of establishing a school to educate children, not just with secular, bread winning skills but a wholesome education that taught the right spiritual values to produce conscientious human beings. This goal, coupled with the wish to provide education for the poor and needy who otherwise could not afford it, led to the founding of the Hariharananda Balashram.

Like any other selfless wish of Baba, this did not take much time to materialize. The search for the school campus in a rural area unpolluted by the modern media, and with a serene atmosphere in the lap of the nature, ended in a quiet solitary corner of the hamlet of Arua, a town full of banana groves and palm trees.

Arua happened to be the maternal home of Mother Vaidehi (Baba's mother), where she grew up before she married Niranjan Dash of Pattamundai. It is also a place that Baba visited as a child when Mother Vaidehi went to visit her maternal home. Much of the farmland on which the Balashram now stands was a generous donation from Baba's maternal great aunt. Such was the detachment, devotion and the generosity of the family that gave the start to this noble mission.

I vividly remember my first visit to Balashram with Harinath in the first year of its conception. I had been hearing about it for some time and it was very exciting to be visiting. We were in Odisha from July through September 2004 when Baba was in residence for the second brahmachari training program at Hariharananda Gurukulam, Balighai. During that time we had the opportunity to visit the Hariharananda Balashram, which is a five to six hour drive from the Gurukulam. Most of the way is a highway except for the last twenty kilometers that go through rural areas and take more time.

On our way, we stopped at the Prajnana Mission, which is also known as the Cuttack ashram, two hours by road from the Gurukulam. We left around 8 a.m. from Cuttack and headed to Balashram.

The countryside in that area is unspoiled and beautiful, and we passed through vast expanses of green paddy fields, palm trees and banana groves so seemingly limitless that you begin to wonder if there is anything beyond them. As we meandered through the narrow mud roads, we suddenly came upon a building surrounded by greenery and more banana groves. It was thrilling to see the small building that housed the beginning of a great dream - a free residential school for children of the poorest section of rural Odisha, who otherwise could not afford even basic primary education.

As we got closer, we could see the children in the playground, little ones ranging from four to five years in age, both boys and girls dressed in their uniforms. Their faces looked bright and cheerful. Prompted by the volunteer teachers of Prajnana Mission, they came to bow to the visitors. They were at the most impressionable age, young minds not yet polluted with the ways of the world, pure and receptive, and as Baba remarked, at the right age to begin learning.

I wondered at the gigantic will and dedication of the Master, which made all this possible. I remembered the Divine Mother being described as *icchashakti, jnanashakti, kriyashakti swaroopini*. Baba's vision manifested all these three- a dynamic will, boundless wisdom and diligent action that stops at nothing to achieve the goal, driven by a mission that has only a few beautiful humble monks, genuine in their love for God and humanity.

Over the past few years, each year we visited, there was something more noble to see – Charitable Health Centers, Dental Camps, projects to help the handicapped, Flood Relief work, Youth Orientation Programs, International Kriya Yoga Seminars, Residential Brahmachari Training Camps, Gita Discourses the list went on. Now the Balashram was a reality, a Free Residential School from nursery through high school, with a curriculum of secular education combined with value based spiritual studies, the best gift one could possibly give a child.

My thoughts returned to the little ones, the flowers of Balashram, as Baba called them. Born in different places and different surroundings, they were now under one roof, an abode of wisdom and spirituality, secure under the guidance of a world teacher who had become at once their mother, father and guide. How many could be fortunate enough to get this kind of an opportunity to be molded into young men and women by a loving guru?

We spent some time talking and playing with the children and then visited the building. The building at that time had two separate dorms for boys and girls with separate bathroom facilities, a meditation hall, a couple of classrooms, a kitchen and a dining hall. At its full capacity, the school would house close to 500 students and future plans for school buildings, a library, auditorium, girls and boys hostels, staff quarters and playgrounds were already under review.

Soon it was lunchtime and the bell rang. Washing their hands and feet, the little children came to the dining room and took their seats. Simple but nourishing food was served. It was beautiful to see the little ones with folded hands and eyes closed, taking part in the mealtime prayer. They finished their lunch and went off to take their afternoon nap.

These children had only been in the ashram for a month, away from their home and parents, and it was amazing to see how well they had adjusted. From the narrow limits of parental love, they were fortunate to enter the portals of divine love, which had no limit or boundaries. Whenever Baba visits the children they come flocking to him and find it hard to part with him. The feeling is mutual, as Baba also comments that the company of the pure and innocent children is the living presence of God.

The dedicated work of the brahmacharinis of the ashram and the caretakers helped the school to become a reality. These children were selected by the Prajnana Mission's assessment team, which visited the poor villages in rural and tribal areas, as well as the slums of the cities. They chose those children who truly needed help, after a thorough check into the socioeconomic background of the families. Some of these children had no parents and some had a single parent with little or no income for daily survival.

When they first came to the school, the children were not used to eating vegetables or drinking milk. They would just eat platters of plain rice since that is all they were used to along with a hot pickle.

Many were infested with head lice and had skin problems. As some of the areas were malaria prone, they also had latent malaria problems. It took almost a year of orientation to get them to normal diet and habits and to get rid of the lice. Neverthless most of them were very agile and had a high tolerance to pain and a cheerful disposition.

Within a few months, the hard work of the brahmacharinis had paid off and you could hardly recognize that they were the same kids. They were brought up in such a loving and spiritual atmosphere, and in no time were able to chant prayers and sing devotional songs. The visits of Baba, whom they loved as their father and mother, were the special treats they cherished and looked for. Baba was equally drawn by their purity and love and would find it hard to part from them on his visits.

The construction of the school continued at a rapid pace thanks to the support of the nonprofit organizations of Hand in Hand U.S.A and Hand in Hand Europe, as well as the generous donations of many noble souls. Many volunteers and brahmacharis of the mission worked tirelessly behind the scenes, donating their time and labor. The official inauguration of the school took place that year.

Hariharananda Tapovan

As we were about to leave the Balighai ashram in Puri and depart for Uttara Kashi, Swami Samarpananandaji (who later became the vice president of Prajnana Mission) approached us with a most auspicious assignment. We were to take with us the idols of Lord Jagannath, Ma Subhadra and Lord Balabhadra along with Sudershana. The idols were made from the wood of the neem trees of Balighai ashram, and were to be installed at the Uttara Kashi ashram by Baba in the second week of February. On hearing this exciting news, we postponed our return to Kansas from the 7th to the 16th of February. Swami Samvidanandaji and Brahmachari Sevanandaji accompanied us on this trip.

After a three-day stop at Rourkela to attend Baba's Kriya program there, we boarded the Utkala express on the morning of the 31st and reached Delhi on February 1st. We left for Rishikesh by car and reached there a little past midnight. The stay in the Kailash Kutir at the Sivananda ashram was beautiful, with early morning prayers and a fire ceremony at the Vishwanath temple, meditation at the samadhi shrine of Swami Sivananda, and the Ganga *arati* in the evening.

On the third morning, we left for Uttara Kashi. It is a five-hour drive through the Himalayan ghats as you ascend to about 5000 feet above sea level. The drive is scenic with mountains all around and the Ganges flowing alongside in the valleys, with a few small towns laced onto the mountain slopes.

As we reached the ashram known as Hariharananda Tapovan, which sat nestled in the Himalayan ranges on the banks of the sacred Ganga, the first thing that caught my eye was the little suspension bridge we had to cross to get to the ashram on the other side

Years ago, even as the land for this ashram was being procured, I had a dream about it one early morning in Kansas. At the time, I had no idea of what it looked like except that we were planning an ashram in Uttara Kasi. In my dream, as I sat on the banks of the Ganga, I clearly saw this small bridge with Baba standing near it with wet feet, and I rushed over to bow. I wrote to him about this dream at the time, and in reply I got a picture of the land with the bridge and the Ganges marked on it much like what I had seen. Since then I had been waiting anxiously to see this place and I was finally here.

We crossed the bridge and followed the path along the river to the ashram gate. Through the gate we walked another few meters to the meditation hall. The hall is small, but with a beautiful framed altar and with two little wooden temples on either side, with Radha Krishna and Siva enshrined in them. The altar, framed in two rows, has the pictures of the lineage with Krishna and Christ on both sides and a small shrine for Lord Jagannath in the center. The bottom half has a life sized portrait of Gurudev Baba Hariharanandaji and the pictures of Paramahamsa Prajnanananda on either side. As you look upon Gurudev there, surrounded by the Himalayan peaks with the Ganga flowing down below, you are reminded of the quote of Baba from the *River of Compassion*. "His life was like a stream of the sacred Ganga, flowing down from the great Himalayan heights in spiritual ecstasy, purifying and sanctifying the life of sincere seekers."

Hariharananda Tapovan at the time we visited, had a meditation hall and a few small cottages for the monks, as well as a small kitchen. Plans for expansion were underway. Swami Samvidananda and Brahmachari Sevananda, along with two other local young disciples, resided at the ashram and worked hard looking after the day-to-day activities.

The ashram provides real solitude. Except for the continuous roar of the Ganga running alongside most of the property, more pronounced here than at Rishikesh, you hardly hear anything else.

The beautiful views of the Ganges and the Himalayan peaks are at once inspiring and breathtaking, a perfect place for those sincerely seeking quiet reflection and contemplation. One can easily lose all sense of time and place here.

The winter temperatures were in the teens. The weather changes rather suddenly, with heavy rains that sometimes last for a couple of days. It can turn pretty cold as well, and we had snow on one day. During the mid-afternoon, if there was no rain, the sun warmed up and as the clouds lifted, you would get a glimpse of the snow capped peaks glistening in the sunlight like jewels against the sky. One could walk along the banks of the Ganga or take a dip in the icy cold waters, which was exhilarating.

One could meditate or study and contemplate in the cottage or on the banks of the Ganga, depending on the weather. Baba has named the Shivalinga here, Gangadhara, and it was a great experience to bring water directly from the Ganga for the *abhisheka*. At 6 p.m. there is chanting and *arati* followed by meditation. The day ends with dinner in the kitchen and some quiet study in the cottage.

Uttara Kashi

We had a couple of warm sunny days during our stay. One day we went to the town of Uttara Kashi, which is 20 kilometers away and takes 30 minutes by taxi. It is a small town with many stores and brisk business as it is on the way to Gangotri, a great place of pilgrimage visited by countless pilgrims each year. We shopped for the worship materials and stocked up on vegetables and provisions for the *pratishta* or installation ceremony the following week.

Then we visited the Kashi Vishwanath Temple. The lingam is slightly tilted and is believed to be the original *swayambhu*, a

At Hariharananda Tapovan

self-manifested lingam. The priest explained that a pilgrimage to see this Vishwanath has the same effect as the one to Varanasi, since the rivers Varuni and Asi that resulted in the name Varanasi are present here mingled with the Ganga. The elaborate *arati* around 7 p.m. to the chanting of many Siva hymns was another memorable event.

Close to the Siva temple is the temple of Shakti that enshrines an awe inspiring huge trident pierced into the earth. Legend has it that it is the weapon of the goddess that was used during the destruction of Daksha Yajna by the enraged Parvati, and that the depth of the trident below the earth is not known.

There are many old and reputed ashrams in Uttara Kashi, including the Kailas Ashram, the Tapovan Kutir and the Sivananda Ashram, to name a few. We returned to the ashram after visiting Swami Premanandaji of the Sivananda Ashram. Swamiji is a beautiful monk and a direct disciple of Sivanandaji.

Devi Mandir

As the afternoon was warm and sunny one Friday, we decided to trek to the small Devi Mandir or temple that perched high up on the top of the hill directly behind the kitchen. The *mandir* had a beautiful idol of Vana Durga seated on a tiger. Bending to go inside, I found a single incense stick that someone had left on the floor and looking around, also found a matchbox with a single match left in it. It could be a coincidence, but it is incidents like these that revive your faith in God's compassion. Lighting and offering the incense, we bowed to the Divine Mother – the daughter of the Himalayas who brought us to Her presence on an auspicious Friday. We made it back to the ashram just in time as the rains hit again. Around 8 p.m., Baba arrived from Rishikesh, along with Shuddhananadaji.

Ganga Puja

The Pratishtha

On the 13th of February, the auspicious day of Saraswati Puja, dedicated to the Goddess Saraswati, we were busy from early in the morning setting up for the prayer and fire ceremony in the meditation hall. By 8 a.m. Baba arrived in the hall after a bath in the icy waters of the Ganga, clad in beautiful yellow orange garments and appearing like a walking Jagannath. As he sat there to begin the *puja*, I felt that he was also the Saraswati whom he was to invoke and the Gangadhara whom he was to install. After all, the *prana pratishta* was with the cosmic *prana* channeled through his *prana* or life force.

The fire ceremony continued with the propitiation of Ganesha, the Navagrahas, the Panchapalakas and with Gayatri, Saraswati and Mrityunjaya. At the end of it was the superb moment of the *prana pratishta*. With Shuddhanandaji continuing the ceremony, Baba took each one of the idols into his lap and covering both himself and the idol, installed the *prana* – the vital life energy into them. After the Jagannath *pratishta*, the Gangadhara *pratishta* was also completed. The huge lingam had been transported the year before by Harinath Baba from Rishikesh.

Then Baba performed Ganga *arati*. This was another beautiful ceremony –the worship and *arati* of Ganga. We followed Baba to the river with the *puja* and the *arati* materials, where, seated on a small rock in the middle of the rushing waters, he performed both. The camphor burnt bright and long and Baba sprinkled the Ganga water on all, as we prayed to the greatest purifier to wash away all impurities and to sustain us with the purity of her sacred waters.

We returned to the meditation hall for the concluding ceremony or final oblation. The oblation was performed with the appropriate mantras and protection was applied to everyone there. Baba sat for a few more minutes, reciting beautiful hymns in praise of Annapoorna, Sharada and Ganga and Jagannathashtaka. *Prasad* followed.

Baba brought the Kashi Vishwanath to the Srikshetra and the Puri Jagannath to Kashikshetra. The same reality pervades the Himachala and the Nilachala and the same Jnana Ganga from Kashi flows into the Ananta Sagara at Puri and it occurred to me that it takes a Prajnana Ganga to demonstrate that.

Swami Brahmananda

In June of 2005, we made another trip to Uttara Kashi. This time Swami Brahmanandaji was there. He was spending time in seclusion for a couple of months before we arrived. We had a nice peaceful time and we went on a day trip to Gangotri with him and other resident swamis of the ashram. We had a nice bath in the cold waters of the Ganga and attended an elaborate *puja* at the Ganga temple. It was a beautiful trip.

During this stay in Uttara Kashi we were fortunate to see Baba again. He arrived at Uttara Kashi with a couple of disciples from Australia and went for a pilgrimage of Gangotri and Gomukh, taking along Brahmanandaji, while we stayed back at the ashram. At the time we did not realize that this was to be our last meeting with Swami Brahmanandaji.

Swamiji became ill while on a Kriya program tour, and passed away the following year on April 2, 2006. It was a truly great loss to Prajnana Mission. His devoted life to Gurudev over three decades and his sincere service to kriyavans in particular, and to humanity at large, serves as a great inspiration to all of us.

The Flourishing Balighai Ashram

Each time I visit Balighai Ashram, I remember the first time I stood at the gate of the ashram talking to Baba with a few other disciples. I said then, "Baba, I feel like this place will grow into another Puttaparthi, where people from all over the world will be coming to attend programs." He smiled and replied, "I would like this to be the International Headquarters for Kriya Yoga."

The large meditation hall with a stage and the altar of the Gurus can accommodate a few hundred people for meditation, and is called the Yogananda Dhyan Mandir. It serves as the meditation hall and also as a venue for *satsangs* and cultural programs. Above the meditation hall, there are two smaller halls – one is Shriyukteshwar Library, and the other is the Vyasa Kaksha, which serves as a classroom during the programs.

To the right of the main building is the Hariharananda Sarovar, a beautiful large pond lined with palm trees and hundreds of flower pots. The pond, which was full of weeds, even up to 2003, was improved later to look as it does now. It is the most beautiful spot, with the reflection of the palm trees on a clear sunny day and with stone steps that serve as seating areas around it to meditate.

The thirty grafted avocado saplings brought from Miami seem to have taken to this soil right away and there are also pistachio, almond, and sapota trees, as well as fig trees from Vienna, and most of our kitchen garden is also on this property, growing many seasonal vegetables.

The property on the west side was purchased to add on to the ashram property. This property was originally low and hundreds of trucks of soil had to be added. A road little more than a half a mile long was laid to stop water coming in from other properties. This property ends at the cowshed in the back.

The Health Center opened in the year 2001, during Guru Purnima celebrations in the month of July. In 2002, we added an ambulance service. The health center has grown from humble outpatient only beginnings to a two-story building with a dental unit in place and is planning to add some surgical facilities especially for the care of the eyes. The center also has a path lab. The Health Center serves a few neighboring villages, giving free consultation and medicines to the poor.

The office building Haripada Bhavan was named after the father of Gurudev, and houses the administrative offices and the bookstore. The main road of the ashram runs through most of the property with roads branching off to the right to different buildings. The road is fenced off from the adjoining property on the left for security.

The ashram temple, Deva Mandir, is a beautiful structure, built next to a pond with steps leading to the upper level that houses the deities. The presiding deity is Lord Siva – called Vishwanatha. The Siva Lingam is in the center of the sanctum sanctorum and on the three sides are beautiful marble statues of Radha and Krishna on the left, Rama, Sita, Lakshmana, and Hanuman in the center, and Mother Parvati, the divine consort of Lord Siva, on the right.

Just outside the entrance, on either side, are Ganesha and Kartikeya. On the upper part of the entrance are the *navagrahas* or the nine planets. Nandi or Vrishabha, the bull that Lord Shiva rides is in the outer area directly facing Lord Siva. On the outer side of the inner temple on the three sides are the statues of the Divine Mother in the form of Mahalakshmi, Mahakali and

Mahasaraswati. The walls are painted with many stories of Lord Siva and on the side facing the inner temple, are the ten incarnations of Lord Vishnu.

Daily worship is performed in the temple, and during special festivals there is a more elaborate ritual. It is the tradition of a *gurukulam* to have a temple on the premises, explained Baba, and Gurudev had also worshipped Mother Kali. It is sometimes helpful to worship the external symbols of God, which serve to remind us of our own inner divinity.

The *Yajna shala* –where the fire ceremonies are performed, is to the right of the temple, directly visible from the main floor. Open on four sides, the structure has a pit in the center for the ceremonial fire. The four Mahavakyas are inscribed on the four sides of the *yajna shala* reminding one of the immortal Brahman. In addition to the temple activities, the *yajna shala* is also used for special events like thread ceremonies and weddings of disciple families.

The Shyama Charan Bhakta Nivas named after Lahiri Mahasaya, the reviver of Kriya Yoga in modern times, and the Navina Kali Matru Nivas, named after the mother of Gurudev are two other buildings which have rooms as well as dormitories to accommodate disciples during programs.

The Annapurna dining hall has beautiful paintings. On one side is the painting of Goddess Annapurna, giving alms to Lord Shiva. Mother Annapurna gives not only food for the stomach but also knowledge and dispassion to the sincere seeker who prays to her. On the other side is the painting of Lord Krishna teaching the Gita to Arjuna. Towards the front of the hall is a life like picture of Gurudev sitting in the ashram. The dining hall accommodates 150 people at each sitting and meals are served and taken with prayers.

We also have the Gayatri Nivas that was built to accommodate the brahmacharinis (lady trainees) away from the general public, to give them a more disciplined and spiritual atmosphere. Then comes the Satyakama Nivas, built to house the brahmacharis (male trainees), although the growing numbers required the building of bigger premises.

Cashew nut trees line both sides of the small road that ends at the Yati Nivas, the residence of the monks on the right side. Directly in front, at a distance, is the back of the Shri Guru Mandir, a marvel of architecture, where the physical body of Gurudev was laid to rest and which is now a place of meditation and a temple for the gurus of the lineage.

A path for *parikrama* around the Guru Mandir has huge stone benches to sit and meditate on, as well as the latest addition, The Unity Trail, which contains altars to the revered figures of every world faith. The ashram has some rare flora and fauna and takes care to preserve them.

Deer, rabbits, and mongoose often come up to the Guru Mandir. There are also raccoons, wolves, hyenas, snakes and black buck deer and many types of birds. We also have monkeys visiting the ashram.

The far reaching vision of Gurudev and its fulfilment by Baba both have no comparison. Every nook and corner of the ashram resounds with the names of the gurus and their presence. One can only bow in reverence to the glory of the guru and his divine will, wisdom and action.

Gurudev Paramahamsa Hariharananda

9

CENTENARY CELEBRATIONS
AROUND THE GLOBE

During Paramahamsa Hariharananda's centenary year, which extended from 2006 to 2007, Baba Prajnanananda conducted "A Celebration of Love and Peace," a global celebration in Gurudev's honor, which included more than 108 events, including conferences on world peace and other humanitarian concerns, interfaith forums, and discourses on a variety of spiritual topics.

The celebrations were held in the United States, Australia, India, and many European countries. During this time, Baba traveled tirelessly from continent to continent and country to country, spreading the message of Gurudev's life and teachings. A compilation of all of Gurudev's teachings, which were a treasure trove of wisdom, was published in ten volumes as the *Ocean of Divine Bliss*.

Baba set three goals for the centenary year.

1. Completion of the Guru Mandir – an architectural marvel and a temple of meditation.

2. Publication of the complete works of Gurudev – A treasure house of spiritual wealth.

3. Centenary celebrations in 108 selected places around the globe – to propagate the life and teachings of the realized yogi.

Inter-Faith Forum in Holland

Holland Ashram at Sterskel is a very beautiful ashram. I visited the Holland Ashram during the centenary year for their celebrations. Baba was going to be there on the 10th of August, which was his birthday. We were accommodated on the ashram premises and had the chance to spend some quality time with him. An inter-faith forum, entitled "God is One, Religions are Many," was held in Holland to help promote peace and inter-cultural understanding with spiritual leaders from various religions.

Peace Congress in Frankfurt

A special highlight of the centenary year was the Peace Congress on November 5th in Frankfurt, Germany. Spiritual celebrities of western and eastern traditions, such as Pater Anselm Grün, Pater Willigis Jäger, and many others took part. This unique and significant Congress was meant to support peace, tolerance and mutual understanding among religions - a high priority in present times.

In Australia, extensive programs were held in Sydney, Melbourne, Bisbayne and Canberra.

Losing a Sister

The Chicago centenary celebrations coincided with Guru Purnima. Just before that event, my sister Radha passed away from lung cancer. After our initial combined Gita studies in our twenties, both Radha and I became busy with our lives. Radha and Ravi also moved to the U.S. and settled in Fort Wayne, Indiana, while we were in Chicago. Except for some occasional meetings and visits, we were each occupied with home, children, husbands and work. Interestingly, we both pursued the Gita studies in our own circles, once we had some time. While Radha stayed in Fort Wayne, we moved back and forth from India to the United States a couple of times, and our jobs also took us from Chicago to Cleveland to Kansas, but the study continued at each place.

Fort Wayne is a town with a strong Indian community and Radha started Swami Dayananda's Gita home study program while she was there, completing the three-year course. Fort Wayne also had a strong Sathya Sai group, with which she was also involved. Sometimes we would meet in India when we were both there. Our visits to Puttaparthi continued, but hers were much more frequent than mine, as she became a really ardent devotee of Sai Baba. She attended all major events and really got involved in the *seva* work, organizing outpatient clinics at Parthi during big gatherings.

When we were first initiated into Kriya yoga, Radha and Ravi had also come to Chicago and been initiated. In the late 90's, after we met Baba and were working closely with him, I asked Radha how she felt about opening a center in Fort Wayne and hosting Kriya yoga programs there. She agreed and we drove to Fort Wayne with Baba, where she first met him. Since then there were regular programs at Fort Wayne and I accompanied Baba on most of those programs. Quite a few people were initiated and the center grew.

It was in the December before Radha's passing that we had a really close time together in India. We met in Hyderabad and she insisted on hosting me in her flat. We had a great time talking about spiritual topics – she developed a great interest in wanting to chant vedic hymns.

It was during this time that I became aware of how much she had transformed and really grown. Years of service in the Sai Organisation and her sincere following of his teachings were apparent in the way Radha dealt with people. If there was any little conflict with anyone during the course of a day, she would resolve it before going to bed, either by clarifying or apologizing as was needed. This was a great lesson to be learned, as I tended to struggle with my conflicts, neither resolving nor ignoring them. As Baba also said in one of his talks, a conflict burns a living person and is worse than a funeral fire, which burns only the dead body.

During the same visit to India, Radha and I also took a trip to Puttaparthi together. We had a great time and also talked about Kriya Yoga. She asked me to demonstrate the second kriya breathing, and after attempting it said she was experiencing difficulty breathing and had to practice more. We were both back in the United States by early the following year and she became very busy with a women's shelter project that she had undertaken at Fort Wayne.

The next thing I heard from Fort Wayne on a Sunday morning was not good news. Radha was diagnosed with a deadly type of lung cancer that was already quite advanced. This was hard to digest and I was in denial, but I soon found out that she did not have all that much time. At the earliest possible date, my husband and I flew to Fort Wayne to see her. She received us with a smile. We sat together and she confided that she had a premonition that something was going to happen. One thing she did request of me on that visit. "I do not have much time," she said. "I want you to read the Bhagavatam for me. Remember this and try to do it soon." I promised her I would.

On a morning in the month of July, I just felt that I had to see her. I bought the ticket for the next morning and flew to Fort Wayne. I took an abridged version of the Bhagavatam with me. When I walked in, there she was, looking as beautiful as ever, nicely dressed though rather weak. With a smile, she said, "They have started me on oxygen." Her next question was "Did you bring the Bhagavatam – we have to start right away."

Soon I was reading and she was listening. She listened with such undivided attention that at the slightest detail she questioned or wanted it repeated. She was feeling tired but did not want to take a break. When I saw her condition, I told her that the 11th chapter contained the essence of the Bhagavatam. "Why don't we start with that and we can go back to the beginning later?" She agreed and I continued reading. Her mind was fully focused and she had no other thoughts.

On Friday morning, they took her to the hospital for another check up. In the evening, I went to the hospital. It looked like something was not right. Again she asked for the continuation of the Bhagavatam and I was reading at her bedside.

In the evening the doctor said she did not have much time, it could be a few hours or a couple of days. I called Baba in Miami and he spoke to her. He told her not to be afraid of anything.

Radha was still fully alert and listening to me read. Her children and many other relatives arrived the next day. Her breath started failing as her lungs were not able to function, and the simple oxygen had to be changed to a forced respirator that covered her nose and mouth. She was still listening and we came to a passage where the author said death is also an auspicious event. She repeated the sentence a couple of times and said, "Yes, I want it to be auspicious." I completed the last verse and said the concluding mantra "*Om Namo Bhagavate Vasudevaya*" and she repeated it after me. After doing it three times, I said. "Radha, I did complete the essence of the Bhagavatam." and she nodded.

Soon, the respirator began to fail. People started chanting the Gayatri Mantra. She kept chanting *Om*. She looked like she

With Sister Radha in Fort Wayne

was sleeping, but I felt she was on another plane. Her voice was becoming faint. Soon she became very still, but her face was bright like that of a child. After a few minutes, they said she was no more. It was hard to believe. There was no jerk or movement of any part while the breath left her body. She left with the chorus of Gayatri Mantra resounding and herself repeating *Om* with a very peaceful face, as though she was in communion with something higher. She departed on an auspicious saptami day, chanting the name of God.

Here ended our physical friendship and *satsang*. It was nice that it ended with a *satsang*. We started with the Gita, a practical guide to living, and ended with the Bhagavatam – the divine play of the Lord – Love and only love. Mysterious as it is, death can be beautiful after a life well lived as hers had been, and it is something to meditate on.

Chicago Program

We left for Chicago on Sunday and were there in time for the centenary program. We met Baba before the program started. When I was in tears about Radha, Baba said we had to take her departure as a lesson in renunciation and discrimination. That evening, we attended the centenary program. Girija, my brother Ravi's wife who is also a disciple and lived in Chicago at the time, came along with her sisters who were visiting from India. After the centenary program, they requested Baba to stop for a few minutes at their house for a *pada puja*. Observing their earnestness and devotion, Baba agreed and we drove Baba to Girija's house.

My Mantra Initiation in Chicago

There was some interesting conversation on the way. Baba asked "Sudha Ma, who is your Ishta?" I asked "Why, Baba?" He said "Just to know," and added, "I was wondering who will give you salvation."

I related to him how as a child I was attached to Rama as an ideal, and how I debated between Rama and Krishna when I was a teenager reading the Gita. I told him how later on, I was initiated with the mantras of the Divine Mother by Sri Ramachandra Murthy. Baba just smiled and kept quiet. But that kept me thinking all night and I felt like getting initiated into a mantra by Baba. The next day I expressed my wish to Baba and asked him to choose a mantra for me. He kindly agreed and asked me to see him the next morning, which was Gurupurnima. I was thrilled to be getting a mantra on Gurupurnima – this was in 2006.

In the morning, I took a plate with water, *chandan*, flowers and *dakshina* and went to see Baba. He said, "Here is the mantra, the deity is Rama," and handed me the mantra written on a piece of paper.

I asked "Baba won't you use anything from the plate and make me repeat the mantra?" He agreed and performed a formal initiation in which the guru sprinkles water as purification and then places the hand on the disciple's head when giving the mantra, making the disciple chant alongside. He showed me how to combine the utterance of the mantra with my breath. He also instructed me to remember my mantra in every breath. I was so delighted and immediately agreed. It was a great feeling to be initiated into a mantra by Baba, and I wondered why I did not think of it before.

A Celebration of Love and Peace in Kansas

We were actively involved with the centenary celebrations in Kansas as we were living in Kansas at the time, and were also hosting Baba every year at our home. The centenary celebrations in Kansas were held at several locations - universities, colleges and temple programs, besides the main public event at the Ball Conference Center.

At the invitation of Professor Marla Selvidge, Chair, Department of Religious Studies, Baba taught two classes at University of Central Missouri. "Creativity and World Religions" was the subject of the world religion class of 90 students and "Loving Your Neighbor can Change the World" was the topic for the ethics class of seventy students. The next lecture was at Johnson Community College – Baba's lecture on 'Yoga for Health and Wellness' drew large audiences.

Baba inaugurated the Hindu Temple expansion event, where he thrilled an audience of 300 people of the Hindu community with his inspiring message. "Expansion of the temple is good," said Baba. "But along with that, we also have to expand our hearts and love, to embrace one and all. Through worshipping the forms, we have to go beyond to perceive the formless *brahman* in one and all and everywhere."

The main centenary event at the Ball Conference Center was a work of art and love by the Kansas kriyavans. The Conference Center in Olathe, Kansas, was a scene of festivity traditionally decorated with *rangoli*, flowers and *kalasas* everywhere. The dais was another work of art, set against the backdrop of the banner "A Celebration of Love and Peace" draped on either side with orange and gold silks alternating with colorful flower garlands. A photo exhibition displayed the many educational and charitable activities of the mission and our many publications.

The conference center was filled to capacity. The event had tremendous public support with The Hindu Temple of Kansas City, University of Central Missouri, and CRES co-sponsoring the event, showing their love and reverence for Gurudev and his teachings. A special feature of this celebration was the participation of the students of religious studies from local universities and colleges, along with their professors.

Centenary Programs in India

After a hectic schedule of programs in the West, Baba was in India in December for the programs there. I decided to attend some of them. I left Kansas on the 30th of December and reached Hyderabad on the 1st of January. After a brief stay there, I left for the Bhubaneshwar program.

Bhubaneswar

The inauguration of the centenary in the state capital of Odisha was a grand success. The huge auditorium was full of people who came to pay their respects to Gurudev and to listen to Baba. The three days went by quickly with talks, initiations, guided meditations and discourses.

In the midst of it all, Baba found a minute here and a minute there to share his love. I found a few memorable moments to be with him and sit at his feet. At the end of the program, Baba left for Cuttack, while we proceeded to Balighai for the IIKYS.

Puri

The 14th was the inauguration of IIKYs on Makara Sankranti day. Makara Sankranti marks the beginning of Uttarayana, considered a very auspicious time when the sun is in the northern hemisphere. I got up at 4 a.m. and after a visit to the ashram temple, went to Baba's room for *darshan*. Fortunately, he was there. I went in and bowed to him, giving him a *tulsi* leaf. He blessed me and ate half the leaf and gave me the rest as *prasad*. I was overjoyed that I could offer him something on that auspicious day.

During the program, Baba talked mostly about Gurudev and his life and message. He also commented on how the ashram had grown in the past 8 years – a tremendous growth and metamorphosis. He reminded everyone that external growth has to be accompanied by a similar inner transformation in spiritual life.

Balashram

Following the IIKYS was the centenary program at Balashram, our free residential school for children in Arua. The arrangements were elaborate and the program was very successful. Balashram represented Baba's dream of producing graduates from the school who would be well balanced and spiritually oriented, with a good value system. It was amazing to see the 120 kids that were admitted by then, all chosen from very poor backgrounds, performing music and dance and doing well in school. The entire cultural program on all three days was put on by the students. One could see how happy Baba was at the school, like a child among children. After the Balashram program, I went back to Cuttack to complete the Sthita Prajna work and then continued on to Bangalore.

Bangalore

The Bangalore centenary program was one of great festivity and the vibrant culture of South India was reflected in its traditional welcomes and Vedic chants at every step. Bangalore welcomed Gurudev's centenary celebrations with great enthusiasm and devotion. Besides the very successful Kriya program of lectures, initiations and guided meditations, Baba was invited to talk at several reputed educational institutions.

Lectures and programs apart, the Bangalore program was great as far as the time I could spend with Baba. Each day there was at least some time where a few of us could sit near him as he relaxed. Just being under the same roof with him gave everyone such joy. As busy as he was, he never forgot to say a word to each one. He would go to the kitchen to say a word to the people cooking and serving. Nothing and no one was overlooked. He made it a point to talk to all those who served, and had a kind word for the drivers of the cars. Such compassion and empathy can only come from seeing God's presence continuously in everyone. As a result of his kindness, all those who served did so with joy and not as a chore.

Hyderabad

Baba left for Hyderabad early on February 14th, and I was booked on a later flight. Baba said he would stop by to see my aging parents – this would be his third visit with them. My father was 95 and my mother was 89 at the time. When I first mentioned them a few years before, and requested that he visit them, he did so even though I was not in India at the time. Since then, whenever he was in Hyderabad, Baba made it a point to visit my aged parents. On this occasion, I received him at their home and hastened to make some arrangements to wash his feet and garland him. My brother Srinivas Mohan was there and completed the formalities.

Maha Sivaratri

Maha Sivaratri occurred during the Hyderabad program. The organizers scheduled a full program of initiations and guided meditations on that day. I was reminded of the *sivaratri* at the ashram the year before, with four abhishekas at the ashram temple, and an all night vigil which Baba spent leading *bhajans* and prayers. I was wondering how we could arrange to visit a temple even for a few minutes on such a holy day.

The program continued with 200 initiations and extended past noon. I suddenly remembered our little family temple under a tree in Ameerpet. The temple was built and managed by my brother in law, Sainath, and was just outside his law offices in Ameerpet. I called my brother-in-law, who was luckily still in the office. I asked him if the priest would be available and if a little *abhisheka* could be arranged. He said "No problem, bring Swamiji." We all stopped at the little temple under the tree on our way back. Sai was waiting with the priest and we all performed an *abhishekam* to Lord Siva. Baba gave the *arati* and we stepped into Sai's office. Coconut water was provided for everyone, and to my delight Baba gave me his coconut with a little water left in it as *prasad*. It was an unexpected and extremely delightful reward.

The next day, Baba had lunch at Srinagar Colony, at my in-laws home where I was staying. I had also invited a few disciples and there were also some young men from Balighai. Sandra Ma and Usha Ma were also staying in Srinagar. Some family members and relatives came as well. All together we had a good gathering.

Baba arrived with the yogacharyas and Amit Baba around noon. We received him in the bhajan hall where he gave *arati* to Sai Baba, and then we did a nice *padapuja* upstairs in the front room of the house. When he was eating, he counted the number of dishes and said there were seventeen items. He then called my niece Kiran and said, "In the fruits bag you brought, there is a nice pomegranate I noticed. Please bring it and cut it." Kiran was very happy. As she was serving it, Baba said, "Now it is eighteen items- this is what I was waiting for." In these small ways he made sure people knew he appreciated all that they did for him. He sat at the table after the others finished so he could give the family members company, and served us with his own hands. After lunch, he rested in the opposite flat and soon it was time to go to the lecture at the Yoga Institute in Sanjeeva Reddy Nagar.

The Hyderabad program was another great one- both on the organizational and personal levels. Well-organized discourses were arranged at the Bharatiya Vidya Bhavan, followed by beautiful cultural programs each evening. Having a home in Hyderabad helped me in doing what I could for the program, and in being able to serve Baba a meal. Amit Baba and his wife Soma Ma were also great hosts and I helped in cooking and serving the meals there, which was a great boon. Both Amit Baba and Ranga Rao Baba are very sincere and dedicated disciples. From the time Baba arrived, till we all bid farewell at the Hyderabad airport, it was a beautiful visit.

After the celebrations in India, I went back to Kansas and Baba went to Europe to attend the programs in Sweden, Munich, Paris, and Switzerland.

I went to as many celebrations as I could in the United States, India, and Europe. By the end of the centenary year Baba had indeed achieved all three goals he had set out to accomplish. To me, it was the greatest tribute a disciple could possibly pay to his guru. Thanks to Baba's dedication, Gurudev's name would be immortalized forever.

10

A Year at Balashram

In 2006 during a program in Dallas, Baba asked me if I would like to spend some time at Balashram, but I did not think of it as a serious possibility. On our next India trip while at Balighai for gurupurnima, I enquired how the school was doing. I was told that the school now had two hundred students, that a few staff members had been appointed, and that some leadership and guidance were critical for the school to flourish.

That night when I was pondering over how I could help, my husband said, "If you want to do something, why don't you offer to do it, instead of just thinking about it?" With this encouragement and support, I spoke to Baba the next morning, offering my help. Within an hour, I received an official invitation from the administrator of Balashram. Since they wanted me to stay for at least a few months, I postponed my return to Kansas.

My Time at Balashram

The best surprise I had when I got to the school was when the brahmacharinis said, "We knew you would be coming. Baba had mentioned you might be here." It was a pleasant surprise to hear that Baba had already anticipated that I would volunteer.

What I thought would be a three-month trip ended up being an eleven-month stay. It was challenging to win the confidence of the staff, who were just starting out, and were not sufficiently trained. In addition, I had to deal with the problems that were already brewing between the warden and the staff and the brahmacharinis –they were mostly due to possessiveness and love for the children- but needed to be sorted out. I relied on the trust that Baba placed in me and was gradually able to win over both sides. After a few days of staying at Balashram as an observer, I was given the appointment order as the acting Principal, since the previous principal had resigned.

I enjoyed every moment I spent at Balashram. It was a challenge working with the children. The biggest challenge, however, was to orient the teachers to a residential school. They at first had this idea of being there for just the class time, and then having nothing further to do with the school. I had staff meetings every Saturday and explained how we were all in charge of the children, not just during school hours but twenty four hours a day, since they had no parents to care for them. Slowly it began to sink in.

The brahmacharinis were a great help, and took care of the administration and also doubled as the dorm mothers. Between all of us, we managed to have a well-run school with a timetable in place. The days were hectic with lesson plans, monthly tests, and orientation classes for the teachers. The students were fun to work with. Some of them were incredibly bright and the best thing about all of them was their willingness to learn anything new. I soon had the library functioning and it was great excitement for the older kids, who borrowed books to read and to study.

A Surprise Visit

On August 10th, we wanted to celebrate Baba's birthday at Balashram. We had a school function with a cultural program in progress in the library, when someone looked toward the gate and exclaimed, "Baba is here!" To our great surprise, we saw Baba walking in through the main gate. He paid us a surprise visit all the way from Europe to spend time with the children. He had brought Jagannath *prasad* with him and distributed it to all of us. He gave a little talk and made everyone extremely happy. He said he had to leave right away to go to Puri but promised to return the next evening. He asked me to prepare the schedule for an orientation program for the teachers and all other staff of Balashram.

We had an all day orientation program on the 12th and also for half a day on the 13th. Baba personally conducted the orientation in a most professional way and it was of great help to all of us, as it was the first of its kind. We felt like one great family under his guidance, entrusted with a noble mission.

When Baba was there he asked me, "So when are you going back?" My original return ticket to Kansas was scheduled for the end of August. I felt that if I left at that point, all the work I did would not count for anything. I told him how I felt and said I would stay longer, at least till the end of the academic year. He did not say anything, but I could feel that he was happy, and then he said, "You know, I will be coming back for some time in October. I have not told anyone about this yet." I was happy that I would be seeing him again soon. The next day before he left, I asked him to sit in the principal's seat and bowed to his feet.

Balashram Children at Guru Mandir

Study Tour

In December during the Christmas vacation, we had the annual Balashram Excursion from December 23rd through the 25th. We chose the city of Puri and vicinity- Jagannath Temple, Ramchandi, Konark and Beleswar beaches as the sites of our visit.

Our Hariharananda Gurukulam –Balighai was the main focus of the study tour, which would also allow the children and the staff to be in the divine presence of Paramahamsa Prajnanananda. The excursion was intended to be a study tour for the students, to be familiar with the different sites and the activities of the gurukulam. The children were asked to maintain a journal and draw pictures wherever possible.

After a stop at the Jagatpur Ashram and a quick tour, the children arrived at Balighai around 1:30 p.m. After a good lunch in the dining hall, the children unpacked and rested for some time in the dormitory of the ashram. At 5:00 p.m. the staff and students met with Baba in the Meditation Hall.

The evening was spent at the Jagannath Temple. After visiting the main temple, there was also a visit to the museum attached to the temple. The children had a great time looking at the different displays in the museum and came back to the ashram for dinner and retired for the night.

On Christmas Eve at 6 a.m., the children assembled at the Sri Gurumandir for chanting and prayer. The early morning prayers with the sun rise along the eastern horizon and Baba joining in was quite an experience.

After a breakfast in the dining hall, the buses left for Ramchandi- a place right off the beach. It has a beautiful temple of the Divine Mother and also has a picnic area and access to the beach. After an hour at Ramchandi, we proceeded to the famous Sun Temple at Konark. It is a very beautiful temple, famous for its sculpture, and the children spent quite some time at the various sites while the teachers explained the background history and the stories associated with the temple. There are vast gardens and parks around the temple and we had a nice picnic.

From Konark, we headed back to the ashram with a stop at the Beleswar beach. The group had a great time on the beach watching the waves and getting their feet wet. For most of the children, it was their first visit to a beach and there was great excitement.

At 6:00 p.m., the chanting and prayer was performed at the Siva temple on the ashram premises. After the prayers, the teachers spent time explaining the different mythological stories depicted through the pictures painted on the temple walls. The children spent time around the Christmas tree that evening.

The highlight of the day's events was a cultural program of dance and drama, which the children presented as part of the Christmas Eve celebrations in the meditation hall. There was the recitation of the Gita, there was a drama enacted in English, singing of *bhajans* and Christmas carols, and also the presentation of the Sermon on the Mount. The entertainment was a great success.

On December 25th, the day started with prayer at the Siva temple. After breakfast and a tour of the ashram grounds, the children and the staff of Balashram met Baba in the meditation hall. Baba spent time with them, telling them the story of the birth of Jesus. Each of them also had the chance to bow at the altar and receive a Christmas gift from their beloved Baba. We headed back to Balashram after lunch. It was a great trip.

Gita Classes at Balighai

During my tenure at the Balashram, I managed to attend a few of the Gita classes in February. The brahmachari training course was in session and Baba was to teach the entire Gita in the course of four months. Baba is the best teacher I have ever known. The precision and the clarity of the subject and the conveying of it in his own unique and simple style with apt examples from everyday life made things very easy to understand and left no room for doubt. The three-hour classes each day felt like they were over too soon and I couldn't wait for the next day. I was reminded of the gitacharya in the battlefield who could convey the 18 chapters so powerfully and lucidly to Arjuna. During the time Baba taught the Gita, it felt like the teacher and the teaching became one. He did not think or talk about anything else.

I eventually had to return to Balashram, as it was time for quarterly examinations. By then we were able to find a candidate to take over as the principal and I began making plans to return home to Kansas. March 15th was my birthday and I decided to leave on the 16th of March.

Before I left Balighai, I requested Baba to have one more orientation session for the teachers. He said he would try, and on the 14th of March we received word that Baba would be arriving on the 15th for a short meeting with the staff. I was overjoyed that I would be able to see him on my birthday. March 15th started off with a lot of handmade greeting cards for me from the children and many precious letters expressing their love. The staff surprised me with a gift of the Konark Wheel as a token of their love, and one of the staff members cooked and brought food for me.

Baba on Education

On March 15th, 2008, the staff of the Hariharananda Balashram had the rare privilege of attending the Mission Orientation by Paramahamsa Prajnanananda, the founder of Balashram, and Swami Shuddhananda Giri, now the president of Prajnana Mission. The time was right as the school had just finished its academic year and was about to start the new session from April 1. We had several new teachers join us to accommodate the increasing needs of teaching.

Baba came in along with Shuddhanandaji. He spoke eloquently and at length about the purpose of Balashram and of education. Addressing the staff as his heart and soul and the heart and soul of Balashram he said,

> This institution is special in many ways. We all are privileged and special and we have a special role to play here. Why do I say special? Because the children are special here.
>
> In her introduction to a cultural program, Sudha Ma mentioned that these children are not underprivileged as most people may think. In fact, they are the most privileged. Considering from where they have come on one hand, and what hope they are given here, they are privileged. Those of you who have decided to serve here are like the strong pillars privileged to be a part of this special mission.
>
> Education is commercialized on a big scale. There is a big cultural change in society. The attitude of parents towards children, children to parents, of the teacher to the students and the students to the

teachers have all changed. Amidst all these changes we still dream to have our culture surviving and Balashram is an experiment so to speak to blend our culture with modernity and put it into reality. We added the ashram since we plan to introduce our old heritage to these modern times.

The challenge is that we have to take care of these children completely. We have to help them grow up. The institute is still young. This is an institution in the making - Lots of things to do and also lots of problems to face. A teacher's role is of great significance. ....I request all of you to adjust to your roles and surroundings and let your dreams blend with ours – these children have no other hope but us. If there is a problem, there surely is a solution. If it cannot be solved, then it is not a problem. When we face a problem, we should come to the other members of our family, and try to solve the problem together.

This ashram will be known all over the world. People from many other countries will be coming to visit. We have to develop our skill of communication. This is an English medium school. Let us learn English better and speak in a better way. A teacher teaches and learns simultaneously. Teachers learn all the time. Even now I am still learning other languages whenever it is needed. Let us learn more and more.

After Baba's talk, some of the teachers spoke. It was also a farewell to me, and some of the staff became emotional. It was hard for me to say goodbye to Balashram and to the children who had become a part of my life.

After coming out of the meeting, Shuddhanandaji said to me, "Go home for some time and come back again."

Baba remarked half jokingly, "Are you sure you want to go?" I smiled and did not say anything.

Later that evening, I requested the chance to do a *padapuja*, and Baba granted me those couple of minutes to wash his feet. I had the garland brought from Baldev Mandir for him earlier and also had *rasavali* from the temple that day as *prasad* for everyone.

Early on the morning of the 16th, I left for the airport after bowing to Baba. That was the end of my stay as the acting principal of Balashram, a very challenging and happy stay. I was sure the new principal would take good care of the school.

Literacy Institute

I did come back to Balashram a few times after that. I visited the school whenever I was in Odisha. My daughter Jyothi was now a professor of Literacy at California State University in Fresno. She had a passion for working with children and she came to Balashram along with her department chair to conduct Literacy Institute for a week at the end of January 2009. Baba was busy at the time, but came in for a day to speak with her before the Institute began. Jyothi loved the children and also spent a lot of time with them. She felt they were the hidden treasures of Odisha and was particularly impressed with one of the youngest students at the school. She wrote,

> Beautiful Sheetal: the face of the new India, epitome of everything the Balashram stands for. Sheetal was found on the roadside, an abandoned infant, near a temple in rural Odisha. Eventually, she was adopted by the Balashram when she was three

years old. Her name, Bharatiya, means Indian. It is the name given to her by the school where she now lives and learns. Her name represents the spirit of this school, where each child is considered a precious flame that will spark the new India, one where caste, creed, background and socioeconomic status no longer stand in the way of education and progress. This is the future envisioned by Paramahamsa Prajnanananda, the school's founder, and coming slowly to fruition in the classrooms and the dormitories of the Balashram. As I look into the bright and eager faces of the children who so easily could have been on the streets, struggling to survive, and with no hope of a better future, I am overwhelmed by the achievement that this school represents. Such a noble mission cannot help but succeed.

The Literacy Institute was greatly appreciated by the teachers, who were taught the latest techniques of reading and writing instruction and how to help students think critically.

Mother Vaidehi

During this time at Balashram, we received the news that Mother Vaidehi had left her body. After the passing of her husband in 2002, she had moved to the ashram at Balighai, becoming a mother to all the disciples who visited the ashram. On July 30, 2007, at her own request, she was initiated into *sannyas* by her Paramahamsa son, henceforth becoming Swami Gurupremananda. She continued to extend her loving care and spiritual inspiration to the world family, while being a resident of the ashram.

On February 5th, 2009, in the period of *uttarayana*, with the sun in the Northern Hemisphere, on *magha shukla dashami*, the 10th day of the bright fortnight, on an auspicious Thursday, the day of the guru, around 1:35 p.m., Swami Gurupremananda peacefully left her mortal body, attaining *mahasamadhi* in the presence of her son. Her wish that her son should be present at the time of her departure was fulfilled by the grace of the Lord.

Together with other brahmacharinis of the ashram, I went to Puri where her body was to be buried. The *bhusamadhi* was performed by Baba with all due rites amidst recitation of the Gita, chanting of the narayana mantra, and devotional singing at our Balighai ashram, where the Mother now rests peacefully. The next day Baba left for a program at Amarkantak Ashram.

In many of his later talks, Baba always referred to his mother as his first guru whom he loved dearly; declaring how proud he was to be the child of such a humble, loving and caring mother, who at the same time was simple and disciplined.

Literate Voices Book Project

Jyothi decided to go back to Balashram for a follow up orientation program for the teachers in the year 2011, and we travelled together from California. On the way from Bhubaneshwar airport, we stopped in Cuttack, where Baba was attending the annual initiation program and meditation camp, to meet him for a few minutes.

By now Jyothi was working with many schools in California. Inspired by the service Baba was doing for the children in India, Jyothi founded a nonprofit of her own called Literate Voices. She worked with the most at risk and impoverished children in California, encouraging them to write and to become published

Jyothi with Balashram Children

Jyothi Sharing the New Release with the budding Authors

authors. She trained teachers and schools to work successfully with such children and spoke at national and international conferences regarding her methods. She also published several articles about the work Baba was doing at Balashram in international scholarly journals.

On her second visit to Balashram, Jyothi wanted not only to train the teachers, she also wanted to directly interact with and encourage the Balashram students to learn through personal narrative, and encouraged them to write their own stories. For the entire week she was there, she worked through the whole day, from early in the morning till late at night, dividing her time between the teachers and the students. I stayed with her and helped. It was a great success.

We were able to inspire the children to relate colorful tribal stories. They opened up and talked of many things that lay submerged in their memories, along with their gratitude for what they had now and their love for Baba. Jyothi summed up her second visit eloquently in her own words:

> I've spent the last few days doing what I love best, working with children. I said I want to help them write their own book if they are interested. They are jubilant at the thought and respond enthusiastically that yes, they do want to write their own book. Each day I spend several hours with the children. I teach them literary devices. We write descriptions of each other. They draw and describe their drawings, using color and detail.

> In the afternoons, I coach the teachers, training them on literacy methods and content area reading. In the evenings, I go back to work with the students

during their coaching sessions. The children struggle at first with the concept of family, since many of them are orphans and some are from broken homes. All of them have left their families behind but they eagerly retrieve submerged memories and begin to describe their lost mothers, absent fathers and the scenic villages they have left behind. They describe the new family they have found in their beloved Baba and the loving brahmacharinis and teachers who have comforted them, loved them, and guided them in their education.

As I listen to them talk eagerly about their dreams, each hope for a good education and a meaningful job intertwined with the larger goals of helping those less fortunate, I sit back in awe at their resilience and their generous nature.

I can only believe that these children are being raised and educated in an environment that fosters such an outlook. If this is the atmosphere and these are the noble young citizens of the future that the school is preparing, then Hariharananda Balashram is truly fulfilling its purpose. Baba has shown me with his school what one man can do to help those who have no voice. He has become a shining example for the children as a noble soul who came from a tiny village and went out and conquered the world, but returned to help those he left behind.

Jyothi eventually put a book together with the stories she collected, and the children illustrated the stories themselves. All proceeds from the book continue to be donated to the school.

Many other dedicated disciples came forward and helped Balashram in many ways – through fundraising as well as by working with the children on different levels. Hand in Hand Europe and Hand in Hand U.S.A. were created to help raise funds for the school. An organization in the U.K. came up with annual treks for disciples to various pilgrimage sites with Baba, which raised quite a substantial amount of money for the finances of Balashram. Though it was physically challenging, Baba completed these treks to raise money for this project that was so dear to his heart.

11

VANAPRASTHA ASHRAM

In our eagerness to progress spiritually, we kept asking Baba how we could proceed to a higher stage. Finally, in 2006, he told us we were ready to enter *vanaprastha*.

Four Stages of Life

Thousands of years ago, the sages of ancient India meditated intensely on the human condition, and determined that there were four distinct stages that men and women should abide by to live the fullest, most rewarding life, one that provides for individual happiness as well as social harmony, for neither can exist without the other.

Stage I- *Brahmacharya*

The *rishis* knew in their wisdom that youth is full of curiosity and unsated desire, and that the young mind is quick to learn, to absorb, and to understand. Therefore, they determined that the first stage of life, a period of twenty-five years, based on an estimated total life span of 100 years, should be spent in exploring the world and gaining knowledge.

Education is of primary importance in this stage of life. Children learn from their parents, their teachers, their peers, and their experiences. It is the perfect time for spiritual instruction, character development, and moral values as well, which along with academic knowledge and life skills, serves to help the individual survive and succeed in the larger world.

Stage II- *Grihastha*

From 25 to 50, the *rishis* felt, would be best spent finding someone to share life with, to indulge in physical and sensory pleasures within the social and moral construct of marriage, and to raise a family. During this stage, one must apply all the skills and knowledge gained in the first stage, and build a home, a career, and a legacy for future generations. The householder is responsible not only for his or her own health, wealth and happiness, but for that of the older generation as well as the younger.

Ambition, hard work, and perseverance are the trademarks of this stage. At the peak of one's strength, vitality and energy, one must work within society for the family and as a result, for the perpetuation of tradition, a moral code, and the flourishing of trade, commerce and individual/social prosperity.

Stage III-*Vanaprastha*

From 50-75 is the third stage of life, meant for a gradual relinquishing of responsibility to the next generation. Kings would hand over their kingdoms to their young heirs at that stage and head off to the forest or *vana*, in order to live a life of contemplation. The sages knew that even for the common man, hanging on too long to one's power often resulted in sons turning on their fathers in a joint family system. They advised the *grihastha* to move on graciously and allow the younger generation to take hold, ensuring that there would be no resentment and that the young would then take care of the old.

Whether one retreats to an ashram or a forest, or lives on within the family home, the focus at this stage becomes social service and spiritual growth through study and meditation.

Stage IV-*Sannyasa*

From 75-100, the final years are to be spent in relinquishing any lingering attachments and dedicating one's time wholly to spiritual progress. Not everyone is able to cut all worldly ties, or spend time in solitude, but the idea is to retreat from the world as much as possible, and to spend most of one's time in prayer and meditation.

The focus at this stage turns inward to the self and the soul. No longer distracted by gaining knowledge, indulging passion, pursuing dreams or even serving others, the individual must strive to know who they are, to understand their inner essence and become one with the Universe.

We were thrilled to hear that our Guru felt we were ready for the third stage. He gave us clear instructions on what we needed to do to prepare.

1. He urged us to focus on giving back to society, socially as well as spiritually, and to live a spiritually conscious life. He asked us to think constantly about how we could serve.

2. He suggested that we read the *Gita* and other good books, and discuss them with each other.

3. He warned us to get over any lingering attachments to me and mine, and to constantly practice the art of renunciation. He suggested that we try to take a weekend every so often where we could remain in solitude without thought or action, to calm the restless mind. He also asked us to try to give up something we were fond of,

Ready for Vanaprastha

such as sweets or salt, for brief periods of time in order to practice discipline.

4.   He explained that in the *vanaprastha* stage, the husband and wife live as friends, no longer engaging in a physical relationship, and focusing instead on *sadhana*.

Over the next three years, we began faithfully practicing the steps Baba had outlined. We each struggled with some aspects of the rules. My husband had no problem with solitude and meditation, while I tended to enjoy being among people. I struggled as well with discipline when it came to food. I loved salty things and had a hard time giving up salt; Harinath Baba struggled with his sweet tooth.

We agreed to live as friends and moved into separate bedrooms. We had no problem with reading and discussing scriptures since we had been doing that for quite some time. As for service, Harinath Baba continued to work in the temples and I focused on the editing of the Sthita Prajna journal as a way to spread Baba's teachings and serve disciples of Kriya Yoga.

Losing My Parents

In 2008, I lost both my parents. I was fortunate to have them for a very long time, since they both lived to a ripe old age. My father passed away in June of 2008 when he was 97. Father was quite alert mentally, even at that ripe age, but was physically weak. He took care of things to the best of his ability, and except for old age, did not really suffer from any particular disease. Then one day in June, when I was in Chicago for a Kriya program, the news came that Father was no more. He had passed away quietly in his sleep. I could share this news with Baba who was present. For a few minutes, I wondered if I should go to India, but there was not enough time to reach before the funeral.

Mother died just a few months later, in September of that year, at the age of 92. During her last years, she suffered with vision problems that hampered her reading, but she still listened to tapes and devotional songs. She would also periodically have trouble remembering things.

I was fortunate to be with her for a few weeks before she passed away. She was bedridden due to a fall. She was alert periodically, and we managed to have some good conversations about old times.

When I got the news of Mother's demise, I was fortunate to once again be with Baba, this time in Miami. He reassured me both times that it was the right time, and that they were both truly noble souls. It helped immensely to have the Guru's reassurance at that point.

All the things my parents did for us children, especially regarding our education, flashed before my eyes. I couldn't help but reflect on the long past days of my childhood and upbringing.

✳ ✳ ✳ ✳ ✳ ✳ ✳ ✳ ✳ ✳ ✳ ✳ ✳ ✳ ✳ ✳ ✳ ✳ ✳

My Roots

I was born on March 15, 1942, on a hot, sticky summer's day, the eldest child of Bhagyavati and Ram Mohan, in my mother's hometown of Guntur in southern India. Mother had returned to her maternal home for her first confinement but returned to her in-laws home in Secunderabad soon after my birth. I was the eldest of six children, four girls and two boys. I grew up in the town of Secunderabad, a nice quiet town during those times, in the princely state of Hyderabad.

Ruled by a prince or Nizam, Hyderabad was once one of the largest and most prosperous of the princely states of India. It had its own army, airline, telecommunication system, railway network, postal system, currency, and radio broadcasting service. All of the major public buildings that still stand in Hyderabad City were built during the Nizam's reign. He pushed education, science, and the establishment of Osmania University. In September of 1948, the Nizam was deposed by the Indian army and the state of Hyderabad became part of Andhra Pradesh.

In those years, my parents were fairly well off, living in a joint family in a huge two-story building, thanks to the hard work of my paternal grandfather, who single-handedly saved for and constructed homes for all his sons. The family was considered ahead of their time, with three of my four uncles having gone abroad to study, and my father being a postgraduate who worked as an accounts officer in the Indian Railways.

The families of two of my uncles who were abroad, and of another uncle who lived in a different town, also lived in the same house as we did, but in different quarters with their own cooking arrangements. There were a lot of us children growing up together, and the house felt like a small hostel, full of laughter and mischief.

Tata or Grandfather Matta Subbiah, valued education tremendously and was very broadminded. He appreciated all religions and was very philosophical. He spoke fluent English. He was a strict father whose sons loved and respected him. He was very careful with his money, successfully raising a daughter and five sons and sending three of them abroad to study. He was also a very loving grandfather to all his grandchildren.

Nainamma or Grandmother was the greatest *karmayogi*, one who worships through work and the fulfillment of duty, and she was named after Annapurna, the goddess of nourishment.

The name was a perfect fit, since the constant refrain on her lips was to offer food to anyone she encountered, whether relatives or outsiders. If there was an opportunity for her to provide relief to anyone within her reach, she was eager to serve them and provide solace. She would lend a patient ear to all who came to her for advice, and many came to her over the years with their individual burdens and cares. *Tata* was an introvert who was aloof and not too social, but his greatness lay in the fact that he never stopped his wife from doing social service. She was loved and respected by all of her children.

In addition to five sons, they also had a daughter Sarojini, who was the eldest. She was married while very young to her maternal uncle, who unfortunately deserted her, and she ended up living with her parents all her life. Refusing to be dejected or overwhelmed by her circumstances, she was an active person, doing whatever she could to serve the brothers' families, and as a result everyone respected her. She spent her entire life serving her nephews, nieces and their numerous children. She was a strict governess, who monitored the activities of all of us girls growing up, making sure that we were safe, and that we conducted ourselves properly.

A Dedicated Father

A literary person himself, my father encouraged me in many ways to improve in the language arts. He would make me listen to the English and Telugu news every morning and to the Sanskrit news in the evening to pick up new words. During school examinations, he sat with us, testing us and tutoring us in his areas of expertise such as history and social studies and English. After each exam, he would check to see if we got the answers right. He had a lot of pride in us when we did well.

Father was also interested in histrionics and elocution competitions. Occasionally, when we had to perform in a cultural program, he would be the director and train each of us to enact our parts well. His training paid off. I was considered the best translator at school. We were also encouraged to take part in debates, elocution competitions, and recitation competitions, and I won many prizes during my school and college days.

Later in life, he was also a good problem solver. He had a knack of making people talk and would listen to their problems and give good advice. He loved all his children. He was a God conscious person who performed *puja* every day.

A Loving Mother

Mother came from a rich and cultured family as well. Our maternal grandmother was a great devotee of Lord Krishna and our grandfather was a saintly man. He was a *tahasildar* (a senior officer in charge of the district administration) who held a prestigious position, and was well respected. Despite his powerful position, he always had the name of Lord Rama on his lips. They lived in the town of Guntur in Andhra Pradesh.

Mother's family was more focused on the study of the Bhagavad Gita and Vedanta, rather than focusing on ritual. As children, we visited our grandparents with Mother during almost every summer holiday. Although I paid little attention at the time, I do recall that there were marble plaques embedded in the walls of the living room and dining room with key verses from the Gita. The teachings of Sri Ramakrishna Paramahamsa also had a great influence on the family. Grandmother was well versed in Sanskrit and Hindi and was constantly immersed in reading spiritual literature. Both on my mother's and father's side, we were blessed with this wonderful spiritual and cultural upbringing, and we were fortunate that both families got along well.

Mother was a college graduate with a Chemistry degree at a time when most girls stopped their formal education at 10th grade. She graduated from Queen Mary's College of Madras, which was a highly reputable institution. She had many lofty ideals and a strong spiritual background.

After her marriage, Mother started working as a science teacher at Keyes Girls High School in Secunderabad, the same school that all the girls in the family later attended. Mother also wrote textbooks on Chemistry and translated them into Telugu since science books in Telugu were not available in those days. Her books became the textbooks at the middle school level.

Mother was an enthusiastic teacher as well as a great mother, and while very affectionate, she was also a strict disciplinarian. Her favorite deity was Krishna, and I remember how she would celebrate his birthday. We would all stay up until midnight and she had an idol of little Krishna in a cradle. After midnight, we had *puja* and Krishna's favorite butter, curds and sweets were offered. She also sang some good *bhajans*.

As a child, I remember how she used to make me stand on a narrow platform in the house and recite verses from *Rama Karnamritam*. I was good at memorizing, and quickly mastered many verses from the scriptures about Lord Rama and Lord Krishna. I also remember taking part in a Gita recitation contest held by Ramakrishna Mission, in which I learned the 12th chapter of the Gita by heart and chanted it to an appreciative audience.

Mother firmly believed in the power of education. She would try to teach even the servant's children to read and write. She insisted on a college education for all of us girls and we all graduated with degrees. She was also responsible for all of us going on to our postgraduate studies.

We were taught from childhood that God is the only one you can turn to for any success in life and that we should always pray to God and be thankful for all we received. Each year after the annual exams, when the results were out and we knew we had passed, we celebrated with a thanksgiving *puja*. We formed our own *Puja* Committee—no elders allowed—and purchased all the things we needed for the *puja*. We cooked several nice dishes ourselves, performed the *puja*, and offered it to God as *prasad* (consecrated food). We would serve the elders first and then eat. This was an annual affair every summer. During holidays, our favorite pastime (there were fourteen of us at one time including cousins, mostly girls) was to act out scenes from the Ramayana. We would make up our own dialogue based on the stories, and entertain ourselves for hours on end.

I was a voracious reader and we were always provided with good books and magazines to read. If I found a magazine or a storybook, I did not put it down till I finished it. Before finishing middle school, I had already devoured the children's versions of the Ramayana, Mahabharata and Bhagavatam. I was also good at narrating stories. Sometimes I read for *Nainamma* and *Atta* during the hot quiet afternoons when they had time to listen.

It was a lot of fun growing up in a large group of sisters and cousins and despite inevitable squabbles and rivalries, we all got along fine under the supervision of *Atta* and our grandmother. Always a good student, I graduated early from high school at the age of 13 and passed in the first class, and then went on to college. College days were also fun. After I completed a Bachelor's degree in science, I went on to complete my postgraduate study in chemistry, and graduated in the first division with a Master's degree by the time I was 20.

Unfortunately, there was not much time during this period for the study of spiritual books, but the foundation laid at home continued, with some discussions about spiritual topics now and then, together with all the festivals and *pujas*.

I feel blessed to have had such pious and thoughtful parents. They devoted their lives to our well-being and educated us by setting a living example for us to follow. I cannot help but think that my early foundation provided by loving and spiritual parents helped prepare me for the guidance of the guru when he finally arrived.

* * * * * * * * * * * * * * * * * * *

Harinath Baba and I continued our spiritual sadhana even as we faced losses in the family. In 2009, we went to the January retreat at the Hariharananda Gurukulam as we did every year. It was announced that some brahmacharis would be made into monks in February. Suddhanandaji said we should become monks. We laughed and replied that if Baba thought we were ready, then we were certainly willing.

Entering Vanaprastha

The day before the monk initiations, Swami Suddhananda called us and said "Get yellow clothes ready for tomorrow. Baba has agreed to give you *vanaprastha diksha*." Elated beyond belief at this news, we both rushed to Puri to purchase yellow clothes. The next morning, we went through *vanaprastha diksha*, a ceremony where we formally renounced the previous stages and donned the yellow robes of detachment.

Having entered this stage, we ended up moving to the Miami Ashram, living in a small cottage on the ashram grounds. We helped in the ashram seva activities, attended lectures, conducted meditation, participated in study groups and helped with programs, while continuing to work on publishing *Sthita Prajna* each quarter.

Much has happened since then, but to this day, I remember sitting on the porch of our cottage in Miami ashram in the early morning darkness, and looking up to see the most beautiful sight. Two giant palm trees stand side by side, scaling the heights of their own potential, while a full and luminous moon glows steadily between. As I watch, within half an hour, the moon slowly disappears into a predawn light that coolly stretches across the sky from the east, inviting creation to embrace the color of a new day. I am so thankful to be here. Not just to be here, but to live here as an ashramite.

Every morning as I step out of the cottage, I get lost in admiring the beautiful garden through which I walk. The mango trees bow down with clusters of fruit that lightly brush my head, plump avocados fallen from the trees during the night litter the walking trail, whilst the birds innocently chirp their morning chorus. As I reach the meditation hall, I am welcomed by delicate white flowers, gracefully laced with the morning dew. I gently collect about seven of these to offer at the altar and then return along the path to the young *bilva* tree.

Bilva is considered to be a sacred plant and the leaves are considered the best for worshipping Lord Shiva. I take exactly one of them as an offering to the Divine Mother and go on further to make my round. The path is lined with hibiscus plants on either side and these floral clouds burst with pinks, yellows, reds and oranges - some with single petals, some with multi-petals and some with centers known as *panchamuki* or the five faced ones.

I feel thankful that I have seen another beautiful day and that I am still breathing, something Gurudev would always urge us to be mindful of. Listening to the chirping of the birds, looking at the flowers and fruits in abundance gives me a feeling of great joy, reminding me of Gurudev, the divine gardener who spent his life preparing the field for that bountiful yield not only of the flowers and fruits but also of human hearts. He was bent on cultivating them, pulling out the evil roots of pride and ego, and supplanting them with love.

I think also of his farsighted vision of providing us with Baba Prajnananandaji, a guru in his image who continues the plantation with his loving toil, supplying the waters of love, warm sunlight, and nourishing soil for our spiritual growth. Every day, I thank the Lord for all that He has given.

My path takes me past Gurudev's old room. I complete my *pradakshina* or encircling of the room and meditation hall to enter through the rear door by the kitchen and offer the flowers at the respective altars - the red *mandaras* and the *bilva* near the Divine Mother's picture in the dining hall, and the white ones at the gurus' pictures in the meditation hall.

Hibiscus or as we call them in Telugu, *mandara*, especially the red ones, are considered very special for the worship of Goddess Durga. Their beauty takes me back to the days when as children we took turns picking *mandara* in the early morning hours for worship in the puja room.

※ ※ ※ ※ ※ ※ ※ ※ ※ ※ ※ ※ ※ ※ ※ ※ ※ ※ ※

As a child, I remember the big *puja* room, which often formed the center of Hindu households in that day. It was certainly the center of our house and was the focus of all activity. The day started with *Nainamma* rising, always with the name of God on her lips. I remember the names she uttered – Narayana, Hari and Govinda as she woke up to her alarm, set for 4.30 a.m., day after day. She was the first one to take her bath and go into the *puja* room. She swept the room, lit the oil lamp near the altar, offered her prayers, and then lit the kitchen fire. There were no kerosene or gas stoves then. We had mud stoves, which used either firewood or charcoal.

Our paternal aunt, *Atta*, as we called her, was the next to go to the *puja* room. She spent much more time washing the statues and the *linga*, and collecting the flowers to make garlands. Quite an elaborate *puja* was performed every day, but she finished before the daughters-in-law and my father went to bow in the *puja* room. We were all involved in some way or the other with the *puja* and had the habit of bowing to God before going to school.

Atta had the interest and time to tell us many stories and teach us how to perform *puja*. Besides attending to the chores in the house, she regularly attended worship and *satsang* in the temples on certain days. Friday and Saturday were special days. Friday was the cleaning day, when all the pictures were taken out and the puja room was completely washed down, the pictures wiped clean, and redecorated with fresh sandalwood and *kumkum*. New flower garlands were prepared, and when it was all completely decorated, it was a heavenly sight. Friday was a special day for the worship of the Divine Mother. Saturday was considered special for the worship of Lord Vishnu. All gods were worshipped in our *puja* room and all festivals were observed on a grand scale. But I must say, the main deities were the Divine Mother, and Lord Vishnu, who was worshipped as Rama or Venkateshwara.

Navaratri

I grew up with the celebrations of navaratri, the nine-day worship of the Divine Mother, as the biggest occasion in our home. All the other festivals, like Ganesh Chaturthi, Ramanavami, Sivaratri and Deepavali were also celebrated in a grand manner, but navaratri was the most important. During this festival, Mother Durga is worshipped in her three aspects as Mahakali, Maha lakshmi, and Mahasaraswati.

I particularly remember the huge oil painting of the Goddess Rajarajeshwari, towering above me in the *puja* room when I was a small child. This was the painting to which the *puja* was rendered during navaratri. Believed to be an original, it was painted by reputed artists during the time of my great grandfather, who commissioned it. After his death, when my great grandmother moved in with her granddaughter, she brought the painting along with her.

The painting depicts Rajarajeshwari seated on a swing, the seat of which is Lord Siva himself. She is flanked on either side by Lakshmi and Saraswati. Many other gods and goddesses, including Brahma the creator, and Lord Vishnu the sustainer, are in attendance and supporting it all is the great *yantra* of Sri Chakra. This picture always occupied the central position in the *puja* room, with pictures of other deities on either side.

When we were growing up, I remember that *Nainamma* and *Atta* referred to the Goddess as a living entity in the house and all activities in the house were centered around Her. Preparation for *navaratri* began almost a month ahead. The *puja* room and the kitchen were cleaned and white washed especially for the occasion. A priest came both in the morning and in the evening to perform the *Lalitha Sahasranama puja*.

Sri Rajarajeshwari

Navaratri or the nine-day worship of the Goddess is performed in different ways in different parts of the country. In South India, where I am from, people are used to reciting the *Lalitha Sahasranama* and this was also the custom in our house. The Divine Mother in one of her forms as Lalitha was worshipped with the thousand names in Her praise. It is believed that this hymn of *Lalitha Sahasranama* was composed by the goddesses of speech at the behest of the Divine Mother herself. It is said that if a devotee recites this hymn out of pure devotion to the Mother, without any material desire, he will be free from all bondage and attain *brahma jnana*. This worship is also known as *sri vidya*. In this sacred hymn, there is a section that refers to the worship of the Mother as the energy residing in the seven chakras or lotuses. The devotee performs inner worship by meditating on and invoking the Goddess in each *chakra* or lotus.

The evening *puja* was more elaborate. Many kinds of sweets and rice were offered during the nine days. Many relatives from near and far participated by coming on their own with all the *puja* materials and worshipping the Mother. They all believed in the power of the deity. The house became like a mini temple during those nine days.

It is customary to perform *kumari puja* during *navaratri*. Young girls between two and twelve years old are worshipped as forms of the Divine Mother. On the *ashtami* day or the eighth moon, *Atta* had all the girls sit in the *puja* room and we were worshipped with sandalwood paste, flowers, and sweets.

I remember *kumari puja* distinctly. *Atta* told us to stop chattering and ushered us girls, aged somewhere between eight and twelve, into the *puja* room. A delicate musk perfume of burning incense wafted through the air while I looked up at the formidable painting of Rajarajeshwari, flanked as She was on either side by Lakshmi and Saraswati. I was always transfixed by Her benevolent gaze.

I was sitting next to Rajeswari my cousin, who always had a habit of making me giggle, but today we kept quiet, because we knew it was a special, reverential day, and also out of fear of *Atta*. As we sat in a row, cross-legged on the floor in our new dresses, *Atta* rang the *arati* bell and touched our foreheads with sandalwood paste and put little flowers at our feet. I remember her face - solemn but kind, disciplined but loving. The sweets were always the best part, and on *kumari puja* day, they were plentiful.

We grew up amid a rich tradition and were fortunate to learn so much just by watching and observing. Grandmother also used to tell us many stories of past incidents that had happened during festival times. Rajarajeshwari was worshipped as a living deity and there were many instances and episodes of Her power. My grandmother and aunt slept in the room directly beside the *puja* room and at night, they often heard the chiming of anklets. They firmly believed that what they heard was the Divine Mother, stepping off the altar and walking through the various rooms of the house.

※ ※ ※ ※ ※ ※ ※ ※ ※ ※ ※ ※ ※ ※ ※ ※ ※ ※ ※

Expanding the Mission

Baba continued to carry on his Guru's work with a resident staff of 70, which included monks, brahmacharis and vanaprasthis. In India itself, the number of ashrams big and small had jumped to 16, with the major ashrams being the Hariharananda Gurukulam in Balighai, Prajnana Mission in Cuttack, and Balashram, which includes the Residential School, as well as two ashrams —the Matru ashram for women and the Dhyana Mandir in Pattamundai. We also had ashrams in Allahabad, Amarkantak, Uttarakashi, and several in Odisha. The major ashrams abroad included Tattendorf, Holland and Miami, and there were requests from disciples for ashrams in South America, Australia and New Zealand.

Now the branch ashrams were sprouting —Kriya Vedanta Gurukulam in Joliet in the Chicago area was a big milestone. Over a hundred disciples attended the three-day retreat, which was a grand success. A special feature during this program was the inauguration of a Sunday school, the first of its kind in our ashrams. Ankur Vidyalayam was blessed by Baba – with its budding students ages 4-6 and a team of very enthusiastic parent teachers. The curriculum was a comprehensive theme of spiritual and moral education combined with yoga, meditation, and exercises. The plans for the Denver ashram were already underway.

After attending the Chicago retreat we came back to Miami and enjoyed two bonus days with Baba before he left. We had a nice quiet time with just the residents on the 4th and 5th and he left on the 6th. We all went to the airport, bowed, and saw him off through security, watching for as long as we could. As always he made an effort to look for us, and wave one last time before he disappeared. Baba was leaving for India via Israel this time. He was spending the whole of *navaratri* time in Israel so he would be able to see the holy land and have seclusion for navaratri.

12

PREPARATION FOR MONKHOOD

For the inauguration of Kriya Vedanta Gurukulam in Chicago in 2010, we were looking for appropriate entertainment, and I requested Jyothi and her husband Ramesh to attend, and for Ramesh to play his saxophone on the inauguration day. They agreed and flew to Chicago. The program was very entertaining and everyone enjoyed the saxophone. At the end of the program, Baba gave Ramesh a token of appreciation.

Before they left, Baba said to Jyothi, whom he fondly referred to as Durgadevi, "Maybe I should disappear for a few days and pay you a visit." It brought tears to her eyes as she said, "Yes, it is about time. I don't get any chance to see you anymore."

In 2011, Jyothi finally bought a new house, and thought it would be nice if Baba could visit at the end of August, which was the time given for the construction to be complete. When she wrote to Baba about it in June, he told her to keep him informed as to the progress and the date and that he would try to fulfill her wish.

We left for India at the end of June with the intention of returning at the end of August to attend the housewarming. But things took a different turn. Days after my arrival in India, I fell while walking and badly fractured both my leg and my ankle. An immediate surgery was required. I called Baba before being wheeled into the operation theater.

I could not hear clearly, but was able to tell him about the fall and the surgery. I could faintly hear him saying, "I will be praying for you." After I got home from the hospital, Baba called and I explained what happened. He said he would pray for a fast recovery and from then on I would send him an email once a week, to which he always replied. I had the wish to somehow see him and also hoped he would be able to come to Hyderabad but he was too busy. It took almost three months before I could travel, as I was asked to stay off of my foot for several weeks and then wear a cast for another few weeks.

We could not be in time for Jyothi's move and had to postpone our trip. When I wrote to him about our plan of arriving in Fresno, California before *navaratri*, Baba wrote back that he would visit us there for a day or two. We requested that he perform a *chandi havan* during *navaratri* and Baba said the day of *navami* or *dashami* should work.

By God's grace we finally arrived in Fresno on the 24th of September. Jyothi's new house was really nice, and she gave us a warm welcome, preparing a beautiful room just for us.

Navaratri started on the 28th of September and we had everything set up in the study for the *puja*. It was a nice *puja* with *Lalitha Sahasranama* performed morning and evening, as well as *deepa havan* with *chandi parayan* every morning.

Baba'a Visit

By the grace of the Divine Mother, we completed the *navratri* worship without any obstacles and on the 10th day of *vijaya dashami*, Baba was scheduled to arrive. He had written that he would come in the afternoon and we could have the *havan* in the late afternoon on the same day. He also said to be prepared to do it ourselves, as he might be exhausted after the long journey. He was coming all the way from the Balighai ashram in Odisha and that too after a nine day fast for *navaratri*. He would break his fast after the *havan* at our place.

We had everything set up and Baba arrived on time. Jyothi wanted to do a *pada puja* to which he kindly agreed and she washed his feet and gave him *arati* in her little courtyard in front of the house. Baba said he felt very happy as he entered and saw Jyothi in her own house after the many troubles she had and the many temporary places in which she had lived.

After unpacking, Baba said he would take a shower and asked us to have everything set up and ready to start by 4 pm.

It was a beautiful day in Fresno – no rain and just the right temperature to have a *havan* outdoors. We set up the *havan kund* in the back porch with real bricks and sand. As Baba came out, he asked who would be doing the *havan*. When we all unanimously requested that he should be the performer and we would help in reciting, he kindly agreed and took the seat.

He explained in detail what we were doing and how we were praying to the Divine Mother who is in everything – in the piece of land we were on, and in the new house, and how we were invoking Her presence both within our bodies and also outside. He lit the sacrificial fire with a prayer invoking the lord of fire who would be the medium to convey our offerings to all the gods and planets. The *havan* continued, invoking the nine planets, the eight directions, the divine serpents, Lord Ganesha, Kartikeya, Lord Shiva, and the many incarnations of Lord Vishnu.

Then we started the *chandi* with a prayer to the Goddess Durga. I was reciting the *chandi* with Harinath Baba, Ramesh and Jyothi were doing the *samputi* with the *chandi mantra*, and Baba was offering the oblations into the fire. The atmosphere was so divine and peaceful and we almost felt like it was a dream. How fortunate to have the guru come from so far away to be with us on the most auspicious day of *vijaya*, to perform a *havan* to conclude our nine day *puja*. It was just amazing what kind of grace would bring so many factors in time together and how blessed we were to be there at that moment. When Jyothi commented on it, Baba said, "It is nothing but the grace of God. God gives us so much." The *havan* was completed beautifully and then we did the *visarjan*, praying to the Divine Mother, sending Her to Her divine abode and requesting her to come back again for auspicious events.

We had a couple of guests who were fortunate to attend the *havan* and have Baba's *darshan*. We slept with heavenly satisfaction, dwelling on our good fortune at having the whole event come together so perfectly.

The next day continued with the same joy. Baba came to the kitchen to give his company to all of us at the same time – while we were preparing the meals. He would go to his room in between to check his messages and come back to us again. He played with Jyothi's dog Sublime, chasing him in the backyard, and I couldn't help think how lucky the dog was to be playing with a Paramahamsa.

There were some enlightening conversations at breakfast and lunch with Jyothi and Ramesh asking questions and receiving responses. My grandson Nikhil had come home late the night before. Nikhil was initiated by Baba when he was 10 years old and over the years, he had kept up with his meditation. After talking to Baba as a teenager about economic initiatives to serve the poor, Nikhil had been inspired to start an education program for the homeless near his college campus in Davis, California. He grew the organization, Davis H.O.P.E., which spread to several universities in California.

Baba spoke to Nikhil, who was now 23, about his future plans and the possibility of medical school. Baba gave him the advice to keep a clear goal ahead of him and work with commitment and focus.

Preparation for Monkhood

Events took a more interesting turn in the evening. Baba was in the living room talking to Jyothi, and as Harinath Baba passed by commented, "Harinath Baba, you look like a monk in those clothes." We were both initiated into *vanaprastha* three years earlier and had been wearing yellow clothes, but sometimes the clothes bordered more on orange than yellow. Harinath Baba was wearing one such orange outfit when Baba made the remark. Harinath Baba immediately went over to Baba and bowing down to him asked eagerly, "When is that time going to be, Baba?" Very calmly, Baba replied "Next year, on Sivaratri day." Harinath Baba bowed to Baba again with tears in his eyes and thanked him.

Though we had a skype conversation with Shuddhanandaji about having to be ready for *sannyasa diksha* on sivaratri day a few days before Baba's arrival, it was different to be hearing it directly from Baba.

Jyothi was a little surprised and asked "What about my parents, if they become monks?" Baba answered, "Parents will always be parents. I made my mother a monk too." When she pressed again as to why we should be monks when we could live the same kind of life at home, Baba said, "Look, I do not want to be praising them in their presence, but Sudha Ma and Harinath Baba have led a good spiritual life, passing through all stages of life even while struggling, and have come to this stage now. I like them and it is good for them now to pass on to the next step and live a life of even more detachment, totally thinking of God and in pursuit of truth."After that Jyothi said, "I guess we should not hinder them from going to a higher step in life."

Later that night I asked Baba for some practical guidance and went to bed more peacefully. There were still questions on my mind – how would this affect finances, where would we live, how would we live? I told myself we would handle it one step at a time. There would never be a perfect time, and if our guru thought it was good for us, then it was best to just follow it as a divine decision.

The next day, we saw Baba off in the evening after another beautiful day in his presence. The next time we met, it would be for our initiation into monkhood, the life changing ceremony with which this book began.

Baba once asked us in the early years how ready we were to face God at the end of our days. "What will you answer?" he asked. "When God asks you what you have done with all the gifts you have been given, a good family, a rich culture, a spiritual and academic education, and a compassionate guru, are you ready to face Him and answer with no regrets?"

At the time, we weren't sure we were ready. We had indeed been blessed with so much. Had we used our blessings wisely? Had we taken advantage of the spiritual and cultural wealth we had been granted in the form of elders, parents, teachers and guides? Or had we frittered our lives away in the pursuit of temporary happiness and material accomplishments? It seemed to me then that much of our lives had indeed been spent fulfilling earthly duties, but both the guru and the Gita assured us that this was both proper and fitting. I, as a daughter, wife and mother, and Harinath baba as a son, husband and father had engaged in karma yoga, performing our duty with faith in God. But Baba's question urged us to think of what more we could and should do. Now decades later, we felt just a bit more prepared for that final encounter with our Maker.

Having spent the past several years faithfully following our guru's guidance, engaged in service and prayer and reflection, slowly disengaging from the earthly ties and responsibilities which kept us bound, we were prepared to take that next step. By entering the monkhood, and plunging into a life wholly dedicated to selfless service and deep contemplation, we would be even better equipped to answer without regret that we had indeed lived a full and useful life.

Swami Gurupriyananda Giri

EPILOGUE

Life doesn't end once one becomes a monk. In fact, this stage has been one of intense reflection and meditation. It is easy to live in the world without thought. Duties overwhelm us, we struggle for survival, we adjust, we manage, we dream, we accomplish. Often, we wish wistfully for a time when we can be rid of all these worldly thoughts and burdens and focus solely on our own spiritual progress. But now that we are here, it is not an easy task by any means.

For 75 and 73 years respectively, my husband and I have been on this Earth. We came here with our own personal knapsack of past karma and accumulated wisdom and clearly a shared destiny that brought us together to make this journey. From our earliest days, we have been blessed with a long line of illustrious teachers, beginning with our parents. Everyone is a guru in his or her own way. From parent to school teacher to spouse, to child, to friend, to enemy, to spiritual guide, everyone comes into our life to teach us valuable lessons. We have learned sometimes willingly and sometimes unwillingly, but the important thing has been to always keep learning.

I feel we were especially blessed to have experienced each of the four stages set forth by ancient *vedantic* wisdom. There were no shortcuts for us, we had to go through each and fully utilize each stage for our own progress. As children, we played, we studied, and we practiced. As adults we loved, we dreamed, we achieved. As elders, we practiced detachment and plunged ourselves into social service. As monks we need to take all that we have learned and move forward, content at last in the inner wholeness of being that needs no stimulus, and no reward.

Finding the right spiritual guru has been a tremendous blessing. While we were always searching for answers, in scriptures, in mantras, in rituals, in lectures from wise men, it was only after we found a truly enlightened teacher that we have been able to tread a steady path toward our own enlightenment.

We each had our own set of flaws that we needed to work on and conquer. My husband had to work on his temper and his lack of patience. I had to let go of my possessiveness and jealousy. Baba often warned me not to be judgmental. He warned against the urge to justify one's actions and criticize the actions of others. It is something I have struggled with throughout my life. They say that spiritual pride is the worst kind of pride. Feeling superior because we have more knowledge or experience is the surest way to halt or reverse one's moral progress. Rather, it is our duty to help those who are unaware, and to reach out to those who still need help.

Much of what Baba has taught us has been through example. He has taught selflessly for two decades and continues to travel the world bringing joy and solace to thousands of people. However flawed his disciples may be, he continues to be patient and continues to guide them in the right direction.

Swami Matrukrupananda Giri

When I look back at the impact he has had on our own nuclear family, I am amazed at how gradual the change has been and how much progress we have all made as a result of his guidance. We are none of us perfect, but we have benefited tremendously from what we have learned.

Not only did Baba help me and my husband, his patient affection and stern rebukes have helped our daughter Jyothi recover from her terrible past, regain her faith in God, and move forward with a clear purpose. He has transformed her husband from a talented but searching soul, into a noble, disciplined, and highly successful artist whose music is his meditation. He has inspired our only grandson to go forward and overcome his broken beginnings as a child without a father, to aim for humanitarian service and become a physician who can not only heal the bodies but tend to the spirit of his patients. I sometimes wonder, if Baba could do so much for our own family, how many lives he must have impacted across the world and how many people he has transformed for the better.

For us, the last few years have been spent in reflection and self-analysis. When we finally stop running, whether toward things or from things, we cannot escape the hard truths about who we are, where we are, and where we are going. We sit and ask ourselves, have we come far enough? Have we done all there is to do in terms of duty and service? Did we use the life we were given in the most effective manner for the best possible purpose? Are we ready to merge back into the Universal Spirit? Are we pure enough, kind enough, compassionate enough, clear enough and still enough? These are questions that all of us must answer at some point. The sooner we become aware of them, the better chance we have of answering them satisfactorily. With the guidance of a guru like Baba, we are surely on our way.

REFERENCES

BOOKS OF PARAMAHAMSA PRAJNANANANDA

Discourses on the Bhagavad Gita1

Discourses on the Bhagavad Gita 2

Lahiri Mahasaya: Fountainhead of Kriya Yoga

Swami Shriyukteshwar

River of Compassion

My Time with the Master

Yoga: Pathway to the Divine

The Universe Within

Krishna Katha

Rama Katha

Bhaja Govindam (Published as Seek God Alone)

Jnanasankalini Tantra

Only Her Grace

UNPUBLISHED DISCOURSES

Dasha Shloki

Kaivlyopanishad

GLOSSARY OF
SANSKRIT WORDS

Abhisheka	- ceremonial bath with chanting
Advaita Vedanta	- the philosophy of non duality
Akashavani	- a voice from the heavens
Anadi	- without beginning
Aparavidya	- worldly knowledge
Arati	- vesper
Ashthami	- the eighth lunar day
Atmajyoti	- the light of Self
Avatar	- incarnation
Baba	- father, an affectionate way of calling the guru
Bhagavatam	- A holy scripture of Hindus
Bhagavad Gita	- A holy book of a dialogue between Lord Krishna and Arujuna on the battle field of Mahabharata
Bhagavata Saptaha	- reading Bhagavatam in seven days
Bhajan	- devotional song
Bhakti	- divine love
Bhakti yoga	- the path of Divine love
Brahmachari	- one who observes the vow of celibacy and self control, one who lives in god consciousness
Brahmacharya	- celibate student life
Brahman	- God the absolute
Bhusamadhi	- burrial
Brahmajnana	- knowledge of self
Chakra	- wheel or disc, a spiritual center, plexus in the spine and the brain
Chandan	- sandalwood paste
Chandi havan	- fire ceremony of chandi
Chandi mantra	- a sacred formula chanted to invoke the goddess Chandi
Chandi parayan	- reciting the chandi
Chitta shuddhi	- purity of mind

Danda	-	stick
Darshan	-	sight or vision
Deepavali	-	festival of lights
Devanagari	-	Sanskrit script
Dhyana mandir	-	meditation hall
Dhyana Shlokas	-	verses of meditation
Devi Mahatmyam	-	glory of the Divine Mother
Ganesh Chaturthi	-	A Hindu festival to celebrate the birthday of Lord Ganesha
Grihastha	-	House holder
Gurukulam	-	a residential school where the students lived in company of the guru and learnt spirituality and a disciplined lifestyle
Gurupurnima	-	full moon day dedicated to worship of guru
Gurudakshina	-	an offering to the guru
Gita	-	short for the Bhagavad Gita, a holy book of Hindus
Gitacharya	-	teacher of Gita
Gita Jnana Yajna	-	Systematic public discourses on the Gita
Guru Govinda darshan	-	the holy sight of both god and Guru
Granthi	-	a knot
Havan	-	fire ceremony
Homa	-	fire ceremonhy
Ichha shakti	-	the power to will
Ishtha devata	-	chosen deity
Japa	-	chanting of a mantra
Jnana	-	knowledge
Jnana shakti	-	the power of knowledge
Jnana yoga	-	the path of knowledge
Jnanendriyas	-	organs of perception, the eyes, nose, ears, tongue and skin
Jola	-	bag
Jyothirlinga	-	a symbol of Siva as a shaft of light
Kamandalam	-	water pot
Kala pani	-	the dark waters
Kalasha	-	a pot filled with water
Karma yoga	-	the path of action
Karmayogi	-	one who follows the path of action
Karmendriyas	-	organs of action mouth, hands, feet, genital organs and anus.
Kriyashakti	-	the power of action.

Kriya yoga, Kriya	- science of discipline and Self realization through meditation
Kshetra	- the field
Kshetrajna	- knower of the field
Kulaguru	- dynastical guru lineage where the son inherits the responsibility of the guru after the father
Kumari puja	- worship of young girls as a part of navaratri celebration
Kum kum	- red vermilion powder offered during worship
Kusha	- a sacred grass used in fire ceremony
Lavang	- clove
Leela	- divine play
Mahaprasad	- consecrated food of Jagannath temple
Maha Sivaratri	- the great night of Siva, a Hindu festival
Maha vakyas	- the Great Sentences of Advaita Vedanta contained in the Upanishads
Makara Sankranti	- harvest festival
Mandara	- hibiscus
Mandir	- temple
Mantra	- a sacred formula of mystic power used for chanting
Mantra diksha	- initiation into mantra
Mahabharata	- the great epic of the Hindus, which is the source of the Gita, written by sage Vyasa
Math	- monastery
Muladhara	- coccygeal center, chakra at the bottom of the spine
Navaratri	- the nine day festival of Divine Mother
Navagraha	- nine planets
Nara and Narayana	- man and God mythological charectars who meditated at Badrinath.
Pada puja	- worship of holy feet of a saint or guru
Panchagavya	- cow products of milk, curd, ghee, cow urine and cow dung
Panchamukhi	- five faced
Paramahamsa	- literally Supreme swan, a title given to a realized Master who attains a supreme state and can distinguish between real and unreal just as the swan can separate milk from water.
Paravidya	- supreme knowledge
Payasam	- sweet rice pudding
Pradakshina	- circumbulation clockwise
Prajnana	- wisdom

Prana	- life force or breath
Pranam	- to bow
Prana pratsihtha	- to establish the life force
Prasad	- consecrated food
Pratishtha	- to establish
Prayaga	- confluence
Puja	- worship
Pujari	- priest or one who worships
Purana	- literally ancient, mythological scriptures of India
Purusha Sukta	- a Vedic hymn on the cosmic form of God
Rathayatra	- Chariot Festival
Rasavali	- a special sweet made of fresh cheese
Ramanavami,	- birthday of Lord Rama. A Hindu festival
Rudram	- a hymn in praise of Lord Siva
Sadhana	- spiritual practice
Sahasranama	- thousand names
Sahasranama parayana	- chanting of 1000 names
Sahasrara	- the crown center also known as the mystical place of thousand petal lotus
Samadhi	- state of communion with God
Samputi	- compounding a mantra with another mantra or prayer
Samskaras	- traditions
Sanatana dharma	- the ancient way of life
Sannyasa	- renunciation, the 4th stage of life dedicated to God and spiritual practice
Saptami	- seventh
Sat-Guru	- a realized Master
Satyagraha	- protest through Silence by fasting
Satsang	- good association
Seva	- service
Shakti	- energy, a name of divine Mother
Shakti Peetha	- the seat of shakti
Shikhara	- peak
Shivalinga	- a symbol of Lord Shiva
Shivaratri	- The night of Siva
Shloka	- verse
Shravana	- name of a month in Hindu calendar, corresponds to August
Shukla Saptami	- 7th day in the bright fortnight
Siddhi	- spiritual achievement, success, perfection

Snana Purnima	- a full moon day on which the deities in Jagannath temple are brought out for a ceremonial bath in the month of June-July
Srichakra	- a symbol used in the worship of Divine Mother
Srividya	- knowledge that deals with the ritualistic worship of Shakti
Sthita prajna	- one who is established in wisdom
Susushmna	- the central nerve channel in the spine
Saraswati Puja	- a Hindu festival to celebrate the birthday of the Goddess of learning
Saptashati	- seven hundred, another name of the book chandi which consists of 700 verses
Tantra	- a system of spiritual practice
Tantric	- one who practices tantra
Tirtha	- consecrated holy water
Tulasi	- holy basil
Upanishads	- Concluding part of Veda describing the way to Self Realization.
Uttarayana	- the six month period when Sun is in the Northern hemisphere
Vanaprastha	- retiring to forest, the third stage of life of service to society
Vedanta	- last part of veda
Vibhuti	- glory, sacred ash
Vijaya dashami	- the 10th day after the nine day worship of Divine Mother, day of victory
Vijnana	- applied knowledge
Yajnashala	- place designated for fire ceremony
Yantra	- a geometrical shape used in tantric practices
Yoga	- one of the branches of Indian Philosophy, also a way of life to union with Supreme self through its practice
Yogacharya	- teacher of yoga
Yoga shastra	- science of yoga
Yoga Sutras of Patanjali	- classical treatise on yoga by sage Patanjali

REVIEWS

OF

THE ROAD LESS TRAVELED

Riding Along on *The Road Less Traveled*

It seems as if I have been on this *Road Less Traveled* with Sudha from the moment I met her. Swami Gurupriyananda, since I have known her, has spent most of her time bringing happiness to others. This book is only a brief glimpse of her journey with Hari, now Swami Matrukrupananda, toward a very joyous time in their lives. I used to ask Sudha, "Why do you follow the Swami?" And she would answer, "To find happiness." It is gratifying to know that her journey was worthwhile.

Sudha and I worked together on many projects and I came to know and love Swami Prajnanananda also. In 2006, almost one thousand people came to hear and talk to him at the University of Central Missouri. It was one of those moments in time that you never forget. He visited again a few years later and Sudha and I worked to find opportunities for him to talk to people throughout the Kansas City area.

Perhaps I am a little bit responsible for the path that Sudha took. She was taping and transcribing lectures for Swami Prajnanananda. And I recognized something very special in her. I thought that she should be a Swami and I asked her, "Why don't you become a Swami?" She did not answer. But her life answered years later when she and Hari sold all of their belongings and headed for an ashram in Odisha, India some time later.

Swami Gurupriyananda's life is worth remembering. Her life informs women that they can walk the same path as men and discover the power of the Divine Mother in their lives. Perhaps her book will help others to find their own special path to happiness.

Marla J. Selvidge, Ph.D.
Professor Emerita
University of Central Missouri

Jai Guru

I am ever grateful to Swami Gurupriyanandaji and Swami Matrukrupanandaji for giving me an opportunity to know of them so thoroughly.

Swami Gurupriyananda Ma, as I observed her through the years, was like a shadow of Pujya Guruji Shri Paramahamsa Prajnananandaji Maharaj and with a detached attachment through these writings, she has become a torchbearer to show us all, the sunlit path to knowledge, detachment and liberation.

Right from her childhood, she was introduced to the path of bhakthi by her illustrious parents and dear aunt. Her journey was further aided by her in-laws.

I am told amongst all paths to Realization, the path of bhakti is a very tough one. But she has shown the readers how to walk that path. Her being blessed at a young age with a private interview with Shri Sathya Sai Baba to love all and serve all has further reinforced her faith in divinity, allowing her to see the unity in all the Masters she has met and to realize that all the divine forms are a play of the mind.

Coming under the guidance of Pujya Gurudev and his chosen successor, Revered Guruji Paramahamsa Prajnanananda Giri Maharaj has made it easy for this couple to go through the four ashramas of life hand in hand.

We are dedicated to them for creating a synopsis of their experiences in these writings.

Gopalratnam Janamanchi
Director - Singapore Shipping International

For more information and copies of book :

Swami Gurupriyananda Giri, 650- 518-6707

Kriya Yoga Institute - USA
P.O. Box. 964215
Homestead Fl 33092- 4615
Phone- +1 305-247-1960
Institute@kriya.org

Kriya Vedanta Gurukulam - USA
3400, Earl Dr, Joliet, IL 60431
Phone - +1 815-267-8977
www.kriyavedata.org

Kriya Yoga Center Vienna
Pottendorferstrasse 69
2523 Tattendorf
AUSTRIA
Ph +43 2253-81491
Kriya.yoga.center@aon.at

Prajnana Mission - India
Nimpur, Cuttack
India
Phone +916712491724
missionprajnana@gmail.com
www.prajnanamission.org